How to
Design Innovations
and Solve Business
and Personal Problems

BOOKS BY ALLA P. GAKUBA, BSCE, MAS, PhD

Trilogy: motivational nonfiction short stories to teach logic, creativity, new skills, and self-esteem that would change readers lives:

What Is Life? What Is Happiness?
(Book 1)

A Person Is a Product of Time, Place, and Circumstances
(Book 2)

How to Design Innovations and Solve Business and Personal Problems
(Book 3)

Alla P. Gakuba, BSCE, MAS, PhD

How to Design Innovations and Solve Business and Personal Problems

Book 3 in the trilogy: motivational nonfiction short stories
to teach logic, creativity, new skills, and self-esteem
that would change readers lives

Copyright © 2015 by Alla P. Gakuba, BSCE, MAS, PhD
All rights reserved.
Library of Congress Catalogue-in-Publication Data
Gakuba, Alla P., BSCE, MAS, PhD
How to Design Innovations and Solve Business and Personal
Problems. Book 3 in the trilogy: motivational nonfiction short
stories to teach logic, creativity, new skills, and self-esteem that
would change readers lives / Alla P. Gakuba, BSCE, MAS, PhD.
First edition.

pages cm
Published by Know-How Skills, San Francisco Bay,
California, USA;
www.allapgakuba.com

Hardcover: ISBN 978-1-943131-25-9
Paperback: ISBN 978-1-943131-21-1
Kindle: ISBN 978-1-943131-22-8
PDF: ISBN 978-1-943131-23-5
EPUB: ISBN 978-1-943131-24-2

LCCN: 2015904744

1. Self-Help – Creativity. 2. Health, Fitness & Dieting – Women's
Health – General. 3. Politics & Social Sciences – Politics &
Government – Ideologies and Doctrines.

KEYWORDS: 1. Innovations roadmap. 2. Examples of innovations.
3. How to solve problems. 4. How to cure some illnesses naturally.
5. The 3 types of economic system. 6. New global capitalism.
7. President Obama foreign policy doctrine.

First Edition 2015

Book designed by Marian Oprea

Printed in the United States of America

10 9 8 7 6 5 4 3 2 1

To my grandsons Paris and Apollo,

with expectations that they will grow into fine men of dignity and honor who will not live selfish lives, but instead will have a purpose in life and make contributions to society, the country, and the world.

TABLE OF CONTENTS

ABOUT AUTHOR...1

PREFACE...5

A GUIDE TO READING THIS BOOK..11

SHORT STORY #1
Skills Are Transferable from
One Industry to Another..15

SHORT STORY #2
How to Design Innovations...25

SHORT STORY #3
How Innovation "Reimbursement from
Medicare" or, "Medicare Advantage Plans"
Was Created?...39

SHORT STORY #4
Learn New Skills Here: How to
Solve External and Internal Problems..48

SHORT STORY #5
How to Calculate Interest Earned on Money?
Or, Does Money Grow on Trees?..56

SHORT STORY #6
How to Cure Headaches, Migraines,
Peripheral Neuropathy, and Fibromyalgia....................................68

SHORT STORY #7
Nothing Happens by Accident.
There Is Always a Reason for It...76

SHORT STORY #8
Look at the Messenger: Who Is He?
Whose Interest Is He Pursuing?..97

Table of Contents

SHORT STORY #9
Everyone Wants You to Be Stupid. Why?
So They Can Make Money from You........................109

SHORT STORY #10
Comediante or Tragediante?
Laugh or Cry?........................127

SHORT STORY #11
How Did the USA Recover from
the Great Depression of the 1930s?........................132

SHORT STORY #12
When Capitalism Ran Amok and
Brought the Capitalist Economy to
the Brink of Collapse, Socialism
Was Called to the Rescue........................137

SHORT STORY #13
What Is Capitalism, Socialism,
and Communism?........................146

SHORT STORY #14
3 Types of Economies:
Market, Planning, and Mixed........................159

SHORT STORY #15
There Are 3 Types of American Capitalism:
Old, New, and Global. What is Old Capitalism?
New Capitalism? Global Capitalism?........................176

SHORT STORY #16
"Look Through the Window."
Or, Marie Antoinette and
President George W. Bush........................183

SHORT STORY #17
President Barack Obama's
2 New Doctrines........................197

SHORT STORY #18
Why Is the NSA Spying on
All 316 Million Americans and the World?..............219

SHORT STORY #19
Big Scams in the USA That Are
Destroying the American Middle Class,
Seniors, and the Nation..............227

SHORT STORY #20
Why Couldn't the USA Recover from
the Financial Crisis of September 2008?
How Can the USA Recover from
Today's Financial Crisis?..............252

ACKNOWLEDGEMENTS..............265

ILLUSTRATION CREDITS..............267

THE AUTHOR'S, ALLA P. GAKUBA, BSCE, MAS, PhD,
CONTRIBUTIONS TO ENGINEERING, TO NATIONAL
WEALTH, AND TO WOMEN:
The Forces of Innovation...Conflict?..............271

HAVE YOU READ? MORE BOOKS
BY ALLA P. GAKUBA, BSCE, MAS, PHD..............277

ABOUT AUTHOR

o o o

When attending civil engineering university in her native city Odessa, on the Black Sea, the Soviet Union, the author, Alla P. Gakuba lived an ordinary life. She was a shy, timid, and unsure of herself young woman, but a serious student.

Fascinated with life, bubbled with infinite youth energy, and curious about the world, she had read hundreds classic books written by world famous classical writers.

She saw numerous movies, the majority of them international, and went to the theater many times to hear the most popular operas, saw ballet performances, not to mention visits to the drama theatre, the circuses, and philharmonic classical music performances, all from a young age.

She was a dreamer...In her dreams she was anything she wanted to be. Intoxicated by life she imitated her heroes and adopted their manner, language, attitudes, and became as sophisticated as they were.

Then, one cold, unassuming November evening, fate suddenly interfered and changed her destiny. Fate propelled her to live on different continents, ambushed her with life-threatening events and monumental problems.[1] She survived, became stoic, and make many contributions.

Alla worked in 4 countries: the Soviet Union, Rwanda, Tanzania, and the United States; in 3 languages: Russian, French, and English; and under 2 radical systems: socialism and capitalism.

Alla P. Gakuba, received her BSCE from Odessa Civil Engineering University in the Soviet Union; she earned her master's degree at Johns Hopkins University, Baltimore; and she received her PhD from George Washington University, Washington, D.C.

Some of Alla P. Gakuba's, BSCE, MAS, PhD, contributions to: engineering, healthcare, and women:

o She designed alone, one person, a 10-span bridge with 4 ramps, I-95, in downtown Baltimore, over the Patapsco River.

o She found the solution how to design "a spiral" and then designed it for 3.5 miles of the Baltimore subway aerial structure which is considered to be the most challenging engineering design.

o She was the 1st woman to receive a PhD in the Management of Science, Technology, and Innovations field.

o Her dissertation is considered to be in the top 5% among 250–300 dissertations written in the last 15 years.

o In health care, Alla P. Gakuba created several innovations. One of her innovations sparked an entirely new industry. It created hundreds of thousands of new jobs. As it grew, it started bringing millions, and then billions, of dollars yearly in new revenue to many companies.

o Please see more author's contributions at the end of this book. Alla P. Gakuba's contributions to engineering, to national wealth, and to women: *The Forces of Innovation...Conflict?* by Carissa Giblin, article provided by the Society of Women Engineers, *The Florida Engineering Journal, January 2004.*

---

[1] About Alla P. Gakuba's life-threatening events and monumental problems please read her short story # 7: "What Is Happiness? Or, What Were the Happiest Years of Your Life?" in Book 1 (the trilogy): *What is Life? What is Happiness?*

PREFACE

O O O

"If only the younger people had the knowledge, skills, and wisdom of the older ones, and the older people had the energy of the youths—the world would be a utopia."

My grandmother Anna

Early civilizations grew and developed from knowledge, information, and wisdom passed from one generation to the next. Before printing was invented, knowledge was transmitted from older generation to younger through long conversations. This was how the youth became wise and clever, and how the civilization could continue to live, survive, and develop.

There are 3 books in the trilogy of motivational nonfiction short stories to teach logic, creativity, new skills, and self-esteem that would change readers lives:

Book 1: *What Is Life? What Is Happiness?*

Book 2: *A Person Is a Product of Time, Place, and Circumstances*

Book 3: *How to Design Innovations and Solve Business and Personal Problems*

Book 1 and book 2 are precursors to book 3. Readers, after reading book 1 and book 2 become knowledgeable and sophisticated, ready to march to the next step, which is book 3. Book 3 elevates readers to a higher level of human development—creativity and innovation.

What are innovations? A simple definition is, that innovations are just solutions to problems. How to design innovations? Innovations require 3 types of creative endeavors: ideas, innovations, and prototypes, as below:

Ideas: Create idea, that is, find a solution to a problem.

Innovations: Design innovation by transforming the idea/solution into an engineering blue print.

Prototypes: Build prototype from the engineering blue print to see how this innovation looks in physical form and test it to see how it works in real life environment.

"Skills are transferable from one industry to another" is one of *the Laws of Life from Wisdom and Experience* in this book. I made this discovery when I changed my field from structural engineering to health care. Soon, to solve some health care problems, I created several innovations. One of these innovations sparked into an entirely new industry. To create new innovations, both fields (engineering and health care) require the same set of skills: creativity and common sense. In this book, readers learn how to create innovations and solve many challenging business and personal problems.

Warnings: Innovations are not designed in a vacuum. Instead, they are products of outside environments such as economical and political; and are products of the world around. This book contains many stories that educate readers about the world around them: what are capitalism, socialism, and communism; what are 3 types of economies: market, planning, and mixed; how the USA recovered from the Great Depression of the 1930s; how to calculate interest earned on money; looking at the messenger; how to design innovations; and many more valuable skills and information.

One of *the Laws of Life* in the trilogy books is, "Information is knowledge, power, and wealth." Intelligence and skills are learned and acquired only by exercising a mind the hard way—from schools and classes you attended, books you read, plays and intelligent movies you watched, people you met and learned from, places you visited, mentors you observed, and friends you learned from.

"Look through the window" is another story in this book. Unfortunately, today's generation is oblivious to the outside world, they are spending their time "doped" on social media, apps, texting, games, and *Dancing with the Stars*. This book addresses this tragic state of affairs.

When looking through the proverbial window one can see a shocking reality. The world population has exploded to more than 7.2 billion inhabitants, a figure that is growing by 70 million yearly; the USA has a population of 316 million, which is growing by 3.3 million yearly.

Today, the world has only one single system—global capitalism, which is "get rich quick from the thin air" mindset. All of the world's raw resources have almost been exhausted, and an environmental holocaust looms ahead. Eastern countries are rising in power and Western nations are sinking. By 2014 China was the #1 economy in the world, supplanting the USA, which is now #2.

Today, 1 in 2 Americans is living in poverty or near the poverty line; the middle class has disappeared; and the majority of industries have moved to China, India, and other parts of the world where labor is cheap and plentiful. The USA is sinking. It is the greatest debtor nation in the world. It has over $19 trillion in ticking debt. Americans have $17 trillion in growing personal debt and $1.1 trillion in student loans.

How can one live and survive in such a strenuous world? How we can stop the USA from sinking? These epic problems need monumental solutions. At the same time, the younger generations lack the needed knowledge and skills necessary to run their lives and address their personal problems—let alone solve the monumental problems afflicting the USA or run the country.

History has witnessed the rise, fall, and disappearance of many civilizations and empires. Recent examples are the British Empire, which disintegrated in 1947 and the 700-year-old Russian Empire followed by the Soviet Union until its dissolution in 1991.

After reading my book, it is my hope that readers will become more informed about the world around them. They will redirect their wasted time and energy away from social media and toward the productive pursuit of real knowledge and skills that only can be obtained the hard way.

This book elevates readers to a higher step of personal development, it teaches new skills such as creativity and innovation, and in several examples gives a road map on how to design business and personal innovations using the author's own examples of innovations.

Alla P. Gakuba, BSCE, MAS, PhD
San Francisco Bay, California, USA

A GUIDE TO READING THIS BOOK

○ ○ ○

This is a book 3 in the trilogy[1] of motivational nonfiction short stories to teach logic, creativity, new skills, and self-esteem that would change readers lives.

Readers have 2 options when reading these stories. The 1st option is to read in sequential order, i.e. one story after another. The 2nd option is to scan the Table of Contents and choose which story to read 1st.

Readers will notice short, repetitive facts in some of the stories. That was done intentionally to ease the flow of reading, instead of referring readers to different stories for facts.

At the end of each story there is a summary—The moral of the story, which states what that particular story is teaches and what questions it answers.

---

[1]   Book 1 in the trilogy: What Is Life? What Is Happiness?

Book 2 in the trilogy: A Person Is a Product of Time, Place, and Circumstances.

How to
Design Innovations
and Solve Business
and Personal Problems

SHORT STORY

Skills Are Transferable from One Industry to Another

○ ○ ○

Skills are transferable from one industry to another. One can see evidence of this lesson in my personal examples, below, regarding how I changed my mid-life career drastically—from structural engineering—to health care.

Turning a Physician's Office from Red to Black

By accident, I discovered that skills are transferable from one industry to another. One Friday in February of 1985 was my big day—my graduation. That day, I received my doctoral degree.

The next day, on Saturday, my then husband, Chrys, asked me to come to his office and see what was going on. I was surprised; I was the last person in the world he would asked for help regarding his medical practice. I was curious. Why was it such an emergency? I went.

There he confessed that his business was failing; his cardiology practice was in the red. His accounts receivable had over $700,000 dollars in uncollectable debt.

Some collection agencies had already collected a small amount, but the remaining uncollectable amount had been returned back to him.

How the Reagan Administration Devastated the American Health Care System

Desperate, Chrys took a $100,000 loan from the bank to pay for 2 consultants to turn his medical practice around. They spent 3 months in his office but could not find any solutions that would improve his office finances and turn it from red ink into black ink.

The consultants concluded the obvious that everyone knew: the new Reagan administration had devastated the health care industry. They had made drastic cuts to health care insurance reimbursements to physicians.

That was the main reason why all physicians were going out of business at that time. One did not need to hire consultants to repeat those insurance reimbursement facts; everyone already knew it very well. By that time, all of Chrys' physician friends were out of business, and his high-rise medical building was now almost empty.

In 15 minutes, I found 4 major problems. He hit the ceiling and said: "Who do you think you are? A superwoman? Here I have 2 male consultants who, for the last 3 months, could not find anything. And you now have found 4 major problems?"

I did not challenge him. I could only imagine how distressed he must have felt. Shocked by his news, I reassessed our personal family situation. If he closed his practice, as all his friends had, what was he going to do? What job could he get? He had no other skills or specialties, and he was intransigent. He could not work in a group with other physicians; he spent too much time individually with each patient.

I was afraid that he would end up leaving Baltimore in search of work elsewhere. On the other hand, I was a woman, flexible and adaptable to any task or circumstance. I could adjust and work in many different jobs.

There were more problems. For example, we were paying high tuitions for our children's education every year. Our eldest was attending an Ivy League school, and our youngest was in private school. For the last 3.5 years, I had been absorbed with my doctoral studies and dissertation research, and that was why I was completely oblivious as to what was going on in the world around me.

There on the spot, I made a decision. I would put my career on hold and make a sacrifice for the whole family so that Chrys' practice could survive, he could continue in his profession, and our children's education would not be affected. The next day, I went to his office, rolled up my sleeves, and went to work turning his medical practice around.

In order to find solutions to his practice's problems, I knew very well that the 1st thing I should do—to find out the reasons (both external and internal) that had led to his office's bankruptcy. I started learning what was going on in outside world and around me and saw the following.

Before 1984–1985, or before the Reagan administration came into power, the majority of physicians in the USA were "solo practitioners," each of whom had an office with 3–5 employees running their practice. Then, the Reagan administration implemented drastic healthcare cuts, and the results were devastating and dramatic.

Physicians were forced to close their solo practices and lay off their office personnel. Patients, millions of them, were left without physicians. That was why HMOs (Health Maintenance Organizations) mushroomed overnight. Before the Reagan administration, only one state, California, had HMOs.

Now physicians had joined to form group medical practices where they started sharing overhead costs and expenses, while other physicians started working for HMOs, medical centers, and hospitals.

As for mental institutions, they were closed down and ceased to exist. Before the Reagan administration, mental institutions in the USA (as was the case everywhere in developed countries) took care of mentally ill patients for free, with patients living in these institutions permanently.

Now the Reagan administration had closed all the mental institutions in the USA. What happened to the mentally ill? They were thrown out onto the streets. The mentally ill lost their health care, food, homes, and the roofs over their heads. They became homeless and started living on the streets.

What replaced these institutions? The Reagan doctrine offered "a personal responsibility" approach: the families of mentally ill patients had to take care of their family members themselves. But this "personal responsibility" approach to care never materialized, as families had no means to support very sick family members.

Even today, such devastation that occurred to American mentally ill people, can be seen everywhere; there are over 1.2 million homeless people. Just go to any big city, and you will see hundreds of homeless people living on the streets. In cities where you do not see the homeless, it is because in that particular city, criminal law prohibits homeless people from living on the streets. They can get arrested and put in jail.

After I learned the reasons why Chrys and all the other physicians were running out of business, I designed several solutions. The American health care system was in shock, and to survive, it would have to undergo fundamental changes, re-engineer itself from scratch, and become a completely new health care system.

I designed a new economical "flow of operations" for the office, brought new services, established a productive money reimbursement method for the service, and trained his office personnel with new skills.

As for his over $700,000 in accounts receivable that the collection agencies were unable to collect, I collected over $100,000 without ever billing 1 patient for owed balances. I turned his medical practice from red to black and almost doubled his income. He continues running his cardiology practice as a solo practitioner.

Working for Health Care

Now that my sacrifices for my family had come to an end and I had accomplished my goal, I was free to go back to my engineering profession. But I did not. Why? I saw that the health care industry was a trillion-dollar industry, and it needed my creativity and skills. I thought that was where I should work, and I did. Instead of engineering, I went to work for health care, an HMO.

During my first days on the job, some employees were curious and asked me: "That must be a nightmare for you because you changed your profession so fundamentally! From structural engineering to health care, solving business problems instead of designing engineering structures?" I did not notice any difference, and I asked myself, *What is wrong with me? Why do other people see the difference except me?*

Then I realized that in both fields (engineering and business), the methodology was the same, and only the terminology was different. In both fields, the methodology involved finding the correct solution to a problem.

It was merely terminology in each field that differed. For example, in structural engineering, the general terminology included designs of "bridges," "buildings," "roads," and "subways." Whereas in health care, the terminology was "productivity," "accounts receivable," "accounts payable," "employee turnover," and "new revenue generation."

The Creation of Several Innovations in Health Care

A few weeks later, no employee ever asked me again how difficult it was for me to change my profession from engineering to healthcare. Why? During my 1st week in health care, I invented my greatest innovation to date which I called "Project Medicare" or "Reimbursement from Medicare."

I designed a 40–50 page blueprint showing how to receive reimbursement money from Medicare for

Medicare patients who were members of HMOs or any other health insurance plan.

Hundreds of copies of my innovation were made. Today, HMOs (Health Maintenance Organizations), PPO (Preferred Providers Organizations), PFFS (Private Free-for-Service), and MSA (Medicare Medical Savings Accounts) under "Medicare Advantage Plans," or my "Reimbursement from Medicare" are collecting between $120–$140 billion per year.

This is due to my noble innovation—"Reimbursement from Medicare." Why noble? Because I received no money for this my greatest innovation, zero, nil; as in the twist of fate.

The next year, I designed another set of ground-breaking innovations to solve medical laboratory problems, they are listed below.

Innovation #1: Designed *"An electronic display to call patients into the phlebotomy area."* It consists of 2 devices: a computer panel "Electronic Display" and "A Console."

Innovation #2: *"Phlebotomy stations for medical lab."*

Innovation #3: *"New operational flows in the lab."*

The above innovations were so successful that they soon became a standard feature in every HMO lab in every state where that HMO was present.

○ ○ ○

THE MORAL OF THE STORY

Skills are transferable from one industry to another. One can see it in my personal examples above regarding how I changed my field from structural engineering to health care.

The methodology is the same where you must solve a problem; only the terminology is different. Such a transition can be successfully accomplished, provided you have enough information, knowledge, and skills stored in your brain's database to create ideas, design innovations, built prototypes, and then implement your innovations.

SHORT STORY

2

How to Design Innovations

o   o   o

Once I was called to a medical lab to solve some of their big problems. The lab was located in a huge multi-story medical center that served over 700,000 patients. It was losing money and patients, had low productivity, a high turnover of personnel, and constant patient dissatisfaction, and complaints.

Previously, the administration had used many consultants and analysts to try solve these problems. They wrote many pages of recommendations that in the end made no difference.

The layout of the lab consisted of one huge room where all the lab equipment and supplies were located. Phlebotomists were on their feet all day, running to the waiting room to pick up the next patient for service. They processed over 400 patients per day in this big room. There was a lot of stress, pressure and friction, as well as many disagreements and complaints in such an unfriendly and hostile environment. The turnover rate for phlebotomists was 3.5 month.

SOLUTIONS

To stop the lab from losing money, to increase productivity, to decrease the turnover of personnel, and to stop patients complaints, I decided to solve the phlebotomists' personal problems first.[1]

How? I created a professional environment in the lab for personnel and patients that was free of stress by designing 3 innovations for the phlebotomy labs, as detailed below.

Innovation #1:
Designed "An Electronic Display to Call Patients into Phlebotomy Area"

This innovation consisted of 2 devices:

1) A computer panel: "An Electronic Display"
located above the receptionist's window.
Size: Length=5'-00"; Height=12½"; Depth = 4½".

2) "A Console"—this was an electronic device connected to the "Electronic Display" and located next to a phlebotomist in each phlebotomy station. To call the next patient into the phlebotomy station, a phlebotomist just pressed a key (A, B, C, or D) assigned to his station.

Innovation #2:
"Phlebotomy Stations for Medical Lab"

Here each phlebotomist had his professional station, layout in an "H" shape, where shelves were equipped with all needed supplies. Now a phlebotomist does not need to be all day on his or her feet looking for the next set of supplies and running to a waiting room to call 100 patients to his or her station for services.

Innovation #3:
"New Operational Flows in the Lab"

I created a structural design for a new layout of the lab. This new lab design separated the lab into 4 simple logical flow areas: 1) Storage, 2) Processing of patients specimens, 3) Phlebotomy, and 4) Reception and the patients' waiting room.

The above innovations were so successful that they soon became a standard feature in labs in every state where an HMO was present.

Just for my readers to get some general ideas on innovation, I gave a short description of all 3 innovations in the lab, in the above paragraphs. However, only innovation #1, "Electronic Display to Call Patients into Phlebotomy Area" and "a Console" are used for demonstration purposes in this short story. From this point on, let's concentrate on Innovation #1.

Innovation #1: "Electronic Display to Call Patients into the Phlebotomy Area" and a "Console"

How and why such idea was created for this innovation?

This innovation was primarily created, to alleviate the physical exhaustion of the phlebotomists. They were running all day from the lab into the reception room to pick up over 100 patients each and every day. I had an idea—a solution to this problem. I must design an electronic display in the reception area. This display would be connected to consoles located on the phlebotomists' desks.

Flow of patients: when a patient came to the lab to get a blood test, he or she approached a receptionist. The receptionist gave the patient a card with a number on it, and then instructed the patient to watch the electronic display on the wall above the receptionist's window and wait for his or her number to appear on the screen.

Then, the patient was required to remember under which station (A, B, C, or D) his or her number appeared, and then proceed inside the lab to that particular phlebotomy station.

Phlebotomists' services: When a phlebotomist, for example in station A was free to serve the next patient, he or she simply pressed a red button on his or her Console, located on his or her desk, and the next sequential number appeared on the electronic display in the waiting room under station A.

The design of the above innovation was one of the easiest parts of the innovation process because they were under my control. The next 2 parts, acceptance of my innovation and implementation, were beyond my control, as they depended on other people. As you will see below, these elements were almost impossible to overcome. My innovation was in jeopardy.

When I introduced my electronic-display innovation to top management, they were up in arms. To them, my innovation was revolutionary and against the long-established norms and regulations in the health care industry.

The assistant of a president warned me, "Over our dead bodies will you implement your innovation in our organization. We are health care providers. We do not call our patients by numbers. We called them by their first names."

My philosophy was completely different. I strongly believed that patients were more intelligent than that. Patients understand the difference between having an appointment with a physician versus taking a blood test in a lab. Indeed, when seeing a physician, a patient usually wants to develop a personal relationship with him or her, so a physician should call the patient by his or her first name.

The same analogy was not true or applicable for lab services. When the same patient comes to the lab, he or she is not looking to develop a personal relationship with a phlebotomist. Some patients are even afraid of needles and blood.

But, what a patient expects from the lab is to be served by using state-of-the-art technology. That is why using numbers for calling patients into the lab was appropriate.

I strongly believed in my electronic device. I did not give up on my innovation and headed for a collision course with top management.

The electronic display was constantly on my mind and appeared on my papers in the form of several blue print designs. But, my electronic device from a blue print needed to be transformed into physical form (prototype) in order to see and be seen and tested for the lab's needs.

Do Not Reinvent the Wheel

The next step was to apply my 1st rule—do not reinvent the wheel when creating an idea or designing an innovation. Instead, I carried out research to see if anyone had already invented it. If someone did, I would suggest that the lab buy it. If this innovation already existed on the market but was not exactly applicable to this lab's needs, then it would need to be re-engineered, modified, and changed to fit the lab's needs.

Also, I scanned my brain database for any information about the electronic display. I remembered seeing something similar to my idea during some sports games. There was a similar display showing the scores for each of the 2 teams.

When conducting further investigation, I found a company that designed and manufactured this particular display for sports games and called them directly. The cost? Between $700,000–$800,000 each prototype, as a special design.

Who was going to give me such an amount of money just for a prototype to test my idea? Top management? They did not accept my idea, warning me that it would happen only "...over our dead bodies." They would never allow my innovation to come to full fruition, let alone allocate this huge amount of money for my prototype. It was just my wishful thinking. I was a dreamer.

But I did not give up. I was under pressure, searching for a simple solution. Finally I found one! I did not need to buy this electronic display as a whole device. Instead, I could assemble the display like a car—from different parts!

Next, I located the needed parts. Some were from South Korea, some from France, and others from Boston, Massachusetts. In the end, my simple electronic device was assembled in Boston for the price of $4,700 for the 1st prototype. I did not need to ask anyone for this amount of money. The device was shipped to the medical center for installation in the lab.

Soon the director of the lab called me with bad news. My progress with the electronic display was being closely watched by top management. The vice president had called her and warned her not to put the electronic display on the lab wall.

By that time, I was not alone in believing in my innovations. Behind me stood the medical center and the lab. The director immediately reassured me that she couldn't care less about the threats, and that they would drill a depression in the wall (size 6'x2') to install the electronic display.

I suggested that it be done late at night, so early in the morning, when the medical center opened "...they would have to pull the electronic device off the wall." She agreed. It was installed at night.

The Electronic Display Malfunctioned

A day later, the lab director called me again with more bad news. This time, the display, after 2–3 hours had gone wild and was flashing the wrong numbers. I went to the lab, manipulated the display, and it started working fine. But the next day, the same thing happened. Again I spent the whole day playing with the display.

I observed that in the morning, until approximately 11:00 a.m., the display worked perfectly and then from 11:00 a.m. until 3:00 p.m., it started malfunctioning, displaying wrong numbers or no numbers. After 3:00 p.m., the display started working fine again.

I theorized that the reason the display was malfunctioning between 11:00 a.m. and 3:00 p.m. (peak hours) was that it did not have enough electrical power during those hours. It shared the same line with hundreds of computers in the medical center, competing for power distribution.

The electronic display was a powerful device that required much more energy than the computers in the medical center. The solution was that the display needed a separate adequate power line.

I called the planning department for help, asking them to ship overnight a separate generator. The next day, the device started using power from the generator, and the problem was solved.

In the end, all 3 of my innovations transformed the medical lab into a state-of-the-art lab and were implemented across hundreds of labs across the country.

Some people suggested that my electronic display innovation in the labs also has spilled into DMV (Department of Motor Vehicles), which also started using flashing numbers to call the next person in line to serve. I did not check with DMV. But is easy to find out. When DMV started using the number display? If after 1989–1990—it means that indeed they took my electronic display innovation from the medical labs.

How Japan Did Not Reinvent the Wheel

Let's take a look at a classic example of Japan, the nation that implemented the rule "do not reinvent the wheel."

After World War II, Japan was devastated. It had lost its colonial power as an empire, had no oil or raw resources, and its many cities were destroyed from the bombings. Soon Japan recovered, and after World War II, it became a front-runner in technology and electronics, exporting products all over the world. It started outperforming the USA and Western Europe in product quality, durability, reliability, and price.

How did this happen? Japan was a classic example of *the Law of Life*, "do not reinvent the wheel." Japan had no raw resources. It could only survive and prosper on the ingenuity of its people, the support of the government, goodwill, and trade—if it could figure out how to produce products with limited resources and in a much shorter time frame. Japan found this solution.

Japan looked toward the 2 superpowers, the USA and the USSR, one had a capitalist system (market economy), and the other a socialist system (planned economy). Japan could not become a capitalist country with a market economy like the USA was; it was not self-sufficient, had no oil and no raw resources, and had no military defense.

The USA would not have allowed Japan to become a socialist country with a central planned economy either, so Japan solved this dilemma. It did not waste limited resources and time by inventing new innovations from scratch. Instead, it "borrowed" existing innovations, services, and systems and improved upon them.

From socialism, it took many elements of strategic planning, government support, management structures, and education. From capitalism, it took technology and electronics. That is why the majority of Japanese technologies were never originally invented in Japan—they were reinvented. Tech products were brought from the USA or Western European markets and reverse engineered—taken apart, reinvented, redesigned, and improved.

Japan made parts or items that were sleeker, faster, smaller, reliable and of much greater quality and that used fewer resources. They sold these much improved, reliable, and cheaper products back to the USA and across the world. For example, Toyota started as a GM car that the Japanese brought from the USA, took apart, and re-engineered with the same parts but with many improvements. That is how Toyota started as a company.

Prior to this time, reinventing tech products was a major Japanese priority. Today such priorities create problems and concerns. Creative thinking and designing innovations from scratch are almost completely absent from Japanese companies and its education system.

o o o

THE MORAL OF THE STORY

What are innovations? A simple definition is, that innovations are just solutions to problems. How to design innovations? Innovations require 3 types of creative endeavors: ideas, innovations, and prototypes.

Ideas: Create idea, that is, find a solution to a problem.

Innovations: Design innovation by transforming the idea/solution into an engineering blue print.

Prototypes: Build prototype from the engineering blue print to see how this innovation looks in physical form and test it to see how it works in real life environment.

When start designing innovations—do not reinvent the wheel. Always look outside to see if your innovation already exists on the market. If this innovation already exists on the market, then license or buy it.

But if this innovation is not exactly applicable to your needs, you must design and engineer a new innovation that will solve your problems and meet your needs.

---

[1]   Please read in Book 2 of the trilogy my another story, "Risk: To Take or Not to Take? Or, Once You Take a Risk, Your Probability of Success Goes from 0% to 50%."

SHORT STORY

#3

How Innovation "Reimbursement from Medicare" or, "Medicare Advantage Plans" Was Created?

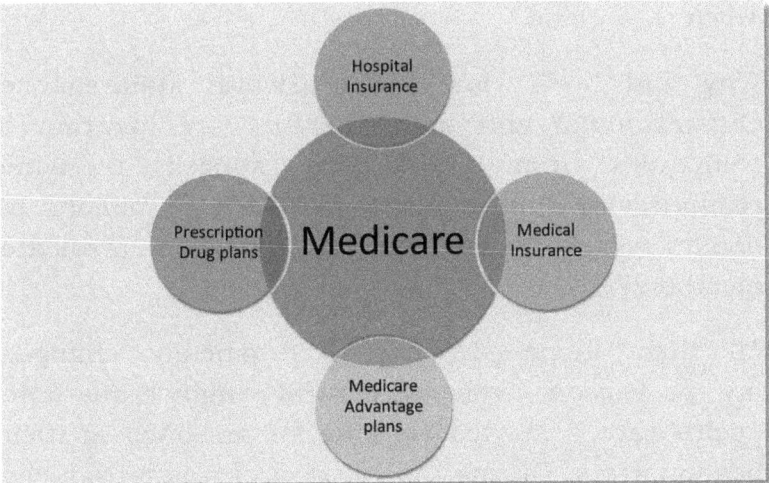

Hospital Insurance

Prescription Drug plans

Medicare

Medical Insurance

Medicare Advantage plans

o   o   o

Medicare was established in 1964 after legislation was signed by the Democratic President Lyndon B. Johnson. From that important moment Americans at age of 65 and older started receiving Medicare health coverage.

But, for the next 25 years, no one in the USA had an idea that HMOs and other health insurance companies could receive millions and billions in reimbursement from Medicare for their members (patients) who were eligible for Medicare—until 1989–1990.

All that because in 1988–1989 I created my innovation named "Reimbursement from Medicare" (originally I called it "Project Medicare"). Later it became "Medicare Advantage Plans."

Why and how? How HMOs (Health Maintenance Organizations) and many health care insurances companies from 1989–1990 started receiving reimbursement in millions and then in billions of dollars yearly from Medicare for their Medicare members?

All that happened when I drastically changed my profession, from structural engineering—into health care. I started working for an HMO in their headquarters. During the 1st week, I was introduced to all of their departments to get to know them and their functions. In the financial department, a chief started showing me his department and described what he and his team members were doing.

When we crossed the account receivables department, I asked him: "How many Medicare patients does your HMO have?" "Oh, I do not know exactly, but probably many hundred of thousands," he said. He was not sure of the number. "Do you ask Medicare to reimburse you money for your Medicare patients?" I continued probing him. "Oh, no, no. We are an HMO, we cannot ask Medicare for a reimbursement. It is a fraud," he answered with some authority.

Coming back to my office, I started thinking about this idea of money reimbursements from Medicare. By the next morning, my idea was formalized. The HMO could ask Medicare to reimburse them for the services that the HMO was providing to each patient. The reimbursement would be huge—in the range of many millions of dollars per month.

My innovation was met with a lot of resistance and non-acceptance. Top management called me crazy. They kept repeating, "We are the HMO here, and it would be a fraud to collect money from Medicare. We are going to be in all the newspapers for perpetrating such a fraud."

I believed in my innovation, stood up, and did not yield, regardless of the hate, name calling, and sabotage. I continued developing my "Project Medicare" or "Reimbursement from Medicare."

To stop my innovation, Medicare experts were called to our headquarters for meetings and analysis to prove that my "Project Medicare" innovation would mean fraud. I expected this kind of sabotage and took the survival of my innovation into my own hands in order to be one step ahead of top management.

I reasoned that if those Medicare experts had my idea, they had almost 25 years, from 1965 to 1988–1989, to create and implement this innovation before me. Why hadn't they? Before the experts arrived, I called them in advance and educated them about my innovation. They agreed with me 100% on the phone.

When the experts arrived to dismiss my innovation as "a fraud," I was ordered not to attend the meetings under the pretext: "You influence people very easily." As for the experts, they also received an order from top management not to talk to me. The experts were 100% on my side, announcing that my "Project Medicare" ("Reimbursement from Medicare") was not a fraud, but rather it was a great and real innovation that could bring millions of dollars to their HMO each month.

Top management made one more attempt to stop me, asking the experts to stay over the weekend, go to some Washington D.C. sightseeing, and to rethink my innovation. The next week, the meetings started all over again. That did not work.

In the end, the result was spectacular. After my "Project Medicare"/ "Reimbursement from Medicare" was implemented, the HMO I worked for started collecting many millions of dollars per month from Medicare.

My innovation became public property. Hundreds of "Consultants in Medicare Reimbursement" mushroomed overnight all over the country. They were teaching HMOs and health insurance companies how to get reimbursement from Medicare for services that they were providing to their Medicare members.

And how was I remunerated for my greatest innovation "Reimbursement from Medicare" that become "Medicare Advantage Plans?" How much money or how many promotions did I receive for my innovation? I received none, nothing, nada, zero. Except, a lot of hate, jealously, sabotage, and dissatisfaction with me.

Recently, there was a TV news story that showed how one HMO laid off hundreds of its employees, because Medicare cut 10%–15% of its reimbursements to them for their Medicare members. Imagine how many thousands of people were newly employed as the result of my innovation.

At this time I learned that in a business organization, it is impossible to create and implement an innovation because of office politics, no manager wants to take a risk or have that responsibility. Let me explain further; for example, let's say you have a great idea and become excited about it, so you take it to your manager and introduce it to him or her.

Immediately, the manager will start thinking about himself or herself. If he or she supports your idea, he or she will take a risk. The manager must ask top management for money and some personnel to conduct a pilot project to see if your idea would work; if your idea is not good, he or she will be blamed and could even lose his or her job.

The fact is: in organizations, no one is punished for doing nothing, but can be punished for taking a risk and trying to implement an idea. The result is that no manager wants to take a risk and toy with employees' ideas.

Remorse

Today, many years later, now that I am wise and experienced, I have huge remorse for inventing my "Project Medicare" (or "Reimbursement from Medicare"). When I started working for the HMO, I was naive and ignorant. My focus was on how to bring in new revenue to the HMO and solve their business problems.

The thought never even crossed my mind about what devastating consequences my innovation would have on Medicare. Thanks to my "Reimbursement from Medicare" innovation, private companies started offering "Medicare Advantage Plans" to patients who have Medicare Part A and B. Private companies: HMO (Health Maintenance Organizations), PPO (Preferred Provider Organizations), PFFS (Private Fee-for-Service), and MSA (Medicare Medical Savings Accounts) where medical services are covered through these private plans.

Then, these private companies are receiving reimbursement from Medicare for their members under this "Medicare Advantage Plan." Amount of reimbursements? Medicare is reimbursing these private companies in the amount of $120-$140 billion per year!

Before my "Reimbursement from Medicare" innovation, salaries of HMOs presidents and top managements were low, below $100,000 p.a. After my innovation was implemented and HMOs started receiving millions of dollars reimbursements from Medicare per month, their top management salaries skyrocketed, from below $100,000 p.a. in 1988 into millions of dollars later.

Today, looking back, I feel remorse and have a lot of regrets. I somewhat partially destroyed Medicare. If it was not for my innovation, today Medicare could have over a trillion dollars more in its treasury. Medicare would not be reimbursing private companies $120–$140 billion per year for their "Medicare Advantage Plans."

o o o

THE MORAL OF THE STORY

Once you have an idea, follow it and think about it. You will be surprised how easily you can formulate the blue print of your idea. Once the blue print is formulated, everything begins to flow in filling in the actual design.

Warning: When inventing something, always think about the consequences (both intended and unintended) that your invention is going to have on other parties, on society today, and for the future. Any invention or innovation always has good and bad consequences.

Today I have much remorse over my innovation named "Reimbursement from

Medicare" that became a private industry—
Medicare Advantage Plans. Which is receiving
reimbursement from Medicare in the amount
of $120–$140 billion yearly.

SHORT STORY

#4

Learn New Skills Here: How to Solve External and Internal Problems

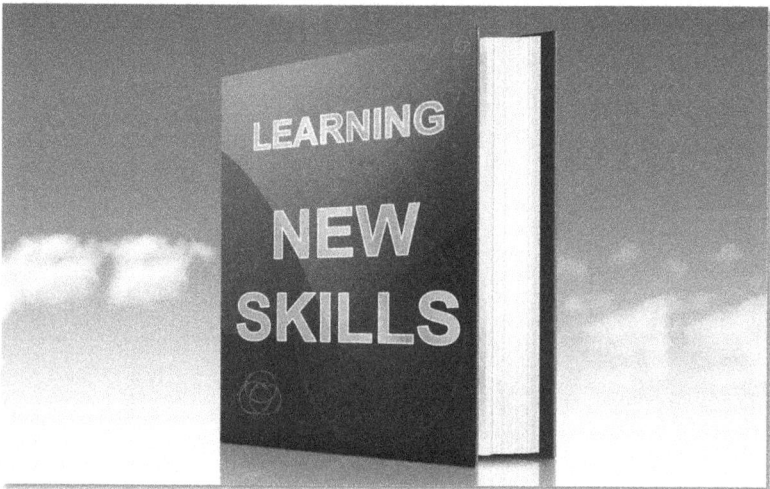

o o o

When I need to solve a problem, personal or business, I employ one set of skills. For that, 1st, I classify a problem by asking: what type of problem is it? There are 2 types of problems: external and internal.

External problems (outside problems)—are *beyond* my control;

Internal problems (inside problems)—are *under* my control.

I feel very lucky and happy when a problem that occurs is internal, under my control. That way, I know that the solution depends on me and not on someone else. I am not going to be at the mercy of another person's whims.

For you, my reader, to understand what I mean by the above principle, let's simplify it with real life examples. Following these examples, you can visualize a problem, understand it, and at the end of this story, you will have learned new skills.

Example #1
Real Life Health Problems

I was referred by my physician for a consultation with another specialist for a medical procedure. I arrived at the scheduled appointment with him. His first sentence to me was: "You must take a risk." Such a statement caught my attention and I started listening intently.

To understand what he meant and make it credible, he gave me an example. He said: "This morning you drove from your home to my office. To drive here you took a risk. On the way here, you could have had an accident. The same applies to your medical procedure. You must take a risk."

I challenged him and explained that driving a car and having a medical procedure had no analogy.

Those 2 actions are different and opposite.

Driving a Car

I agreed with him that when I drove a car from my home to his office, indeed, I took a risk. Was my driving on a highway under my control? No. I had no control (assuming that I was a responsible and defensive driver: no alcohol, no drugs, no texting, and no talking on the phone). On the road, around me, I was sure there were some irresponsible drivers who could hit my car and cause an accident. Their actions were beyond my control. I took a risk driving there and was lucky to arrive in one piece.

At the same time, driving was an everyday need and a necessary act. A car was indispensable to living. Without driving a car, I could not work, earn any money, buy food, pay for a roof over my head, and tend to other life necessities.

Medical Procedure

This was a risky medical procedure. I could have a stroke, a heart attack, or many other complications could result from the procedure. I could be hurt from the side effects of the anesthesia, get an infection, or even be clinically injured. At the same time, this medical procedure was an elective procedure; I could live without it. To solve this problem, it was up to me to make a decision about what action to choose: to do it or not to do it? *The choice about the medical procedure was under my control!*

While driving hazards were beyond my control, I had no choice and had to take a risk and rely solely on luck, hoping and praying that no irresponsible driver would hit my car.

Example #2
Real Life Rental Problems in a Spectrum Apartment Complex

This problem developed during the year 2010: How and why Spectrum Apartments kept losing rent money versus 12 months ago?

Solution: The fact was that rents were in a free fall— all due to 2 types of problems:

A) Internal problems: they were *under the control* of Spectrum Apartments;

B) External problems: they were *beyond the control* of Spectrum Apartments.

A) Internal problems that were *under the control* of Spectrum Apartments:

1) There were high apartment vacancies in Spectrum Apartments due to inflated, above market rent prices. Tenants were leaving and renting from other competitors for much lower, market rents.

2) There was a high turnover of tenants, due to inflated rents, and tenants were occupying Spectrum Apartments for a short time, between 3–6 months. It was documented that in a 12-month period, the average apartment was empty for 2–3 months or longer. The result was: a loss of 2–3 months of rent in a 12-month period for each apartment. The total loss was over $400,000 for the whole complex.

B) External problems that were *beyond the control* of Spectrum Apartments:

External problems are also responsible for current rent losses in Spectrum Apartments versus 6–12 months ago, they include the following:

1) Currently, the USA and the world economies have collapsed: high unemployment was a big issue and the USA has over 14 million unemployed people.

Every month, over 600,000 newly unemployed people join the current rank of 14 million.

2) The USA government has a $13 trillion ticking national debt, yet it has kept printing money and borrowing more from China, Japan, Russia, and Brazil.

3) The population has no money and savings and lives off credit cards: in 2010 with credit card debts over $8,000/per person: mortgage debt over $155,000/per household; and students loan debt over $25,000/per student.

4) High home foreclosures: 1 in 5 homeowners' mortgages were underwater. Over 30 million homeowners owe more on their mortgages than the market value of their homes.

Question: Where were the millions of foreclosed homeowners going? Answer: Having no money, they stopped renting overpriced apartments in California. Instead, some started moving in with their relatives and friends, while others were moving out to other, much cheaper states where apartment rents were 2–5 times cheaper.

The above was not new. Before that, a similar economic situation already existed in the San Francisco Bay area from 1988–1996. For example, in 1988–1996 in San Francisco, a huge house with 5 bedrooms, 4 bathrooms, and 3 car garages next to Golden Park was rented by my young son and his friend for $700 per month.

At the same time, a 1 bedroom/1 bathroom newly built condo in downtown San Francisco had an asking price somewhere around $120,000 per unit. In Maryland, homeowners advertised their houses rent-free (an empty house deteriorates very quickly).

In New York City, the asking price for a 1-bedroom condo in the new high-rise apartments near Bloomingdales department store was $120,000 per unit.

Then, in 1996, Wall Street invented "dot.com" scam and the stock market took off—and so did prices for rent. Renting a house/condo was inflated by 2–5 times the usual cost.

○ ○ ○

THE MORAL OF THE STORY

The new skill you learned from the above story: When solving any problem (personal or business), 1st retrieve all facts and information for your problem, 2nd, separate facts and information into 2 types, one for external problems, another for internal problems, as below:

External problems (outside problems)—are *beyond* your control

Internal problems (inside problems)—are *under* your control

Then, solve internal problems that are under your control. For help and methodology, please see the 2 examples above in this story.

SHORT STORY

How to Calculate Interest Earned on Money? Or, Does Money Grow on Trees?

O O O

"It is better to have one bird in your hands than hundreds of birds in the sky."

Anonymous

How to become a powerful person? Become a saver. Saving money is under your control; here you have power over your money when jobs, and what you get paid, all are beyond your control. Question: How to grow your saved money? Answer: From interest rates. Interest rates were the greatest invention of the 19th century. An interest rate to savers is like money growing on trees.

There are 2 types of interest rates: 1) Simple interest rates, and 2) Compound interest rates.

1) Simple interest rate is interest that is earned only on the principal amount of money

Below is the most important formula in your everyday life; learn and visualize it. The formula is going to be your new skill!

Example A

Nancy deposited her savings of $10,000 into a Certificate of Deposit (CD) for 3 years, at 3% simple interest per year.

In the 1st year, her earned interest =$300;

2nd year =$300; 3rd year =$300.

That is: each year Nancy earned $300 in interest on her principal.

Total simple interest in 3 years = $900 =($300 + $300 + $300).

For 1st year: $10,000 =100%;

X =($10,000 x 3%) ÷ 100% =$300;

X = 3%

Where:

$10,000 – principal and earned simple interest after 1 year

X – find unknown earned simple interest after 1 year

$300 – actual earned simple interest after 1 year

2) Compound interest rate is earned interest on the saver's interest

Example B

Nancy deposited her $10,000 into a CD for 3 years, at 3% interest per year compounded yearly.

1st year Nancy earned = $300 in interest;

2nd year = $309; 3rd year =$318.27.

For 3rd year: $10,609 =100%;

X = ($10,609 x 3%) ÷ 100% =$318.27;

X = 3%

<u>Where:</u>

$10,609 – principal and earned compound interest after 2nd year

X – find unknown earned compound interest after 3rd year

$318.28 – actual earned compound interest after 3rd year

Total earned compound interest in 3 years = $927.28 =($300 + 309 + 318.28).

A Money Saver Is a Powerful and a Creative Person

A wise saying teaches "It is better to have one bird in your hands than hundreds of birds in the sky." Interpretation: It is better to have your money "in your hands"—in your savings accounts (CDs and money market)—than to gamble your hard-earned money and give it to Wall Street fund managers and various financial advisors to manage it.

"Money does grow on trees" is true; it happens when a person becomes a money saver. A money saver becomes a powerful person, his self-esteem goes up.

The 1st step is—he saves money, then these savings are put into a savings account in the bank, money market, or CDs. At a certain interest rate, say 3%–

7% interest annually and without working, his or her money will start earning interest and grow.

Even more, saving money and how much is under a saver's control. A saver does not speculate to increase his money. His profit come from earned interests in money market and CDs accounts.

For example, Nancy saved $10,000 and put it into a CD for 12 months at an interest rate of 3% annually. Then 12 month later, Nancy's money earned $300.00 in interest. Nancy felt great, without working she earned $300.00.

Nancy felt powerful and in control of her money. Her money was safe and was insured by the FDIC (Federal Deposit Insurance Corporation) up to $250,000 in each account. And she had access to her money any time she wanted or needed it.

But, if she gave her money to Wall Street fund managers or financial advisers to invest, she would lose control of her money. It is like a gambler at the casino; she could lose her money any day or any time.

She would lose her power, as she cannot control other people's actions, what they do with her money, or when and how much money she would get back, if any. "It is better to have one bird in your hands than hundreds in the sky," as the wise saying states.

How to Calculate Earned Interest in Money Market Accounts and CDs

Here is the most important simple formula in your everyday life. When you master it—it should become your new everyday skill.

Every morning, a person should think: "How can I save some money today?" It is easy; use your creativity and imagination, and you will be surprised by how much money you can save every day or at the end of the week or month.

Some examples: pack your lunch instead of buying it; to save on gas use a credit card that gives a discount of 3% or 5% on gas; walk, take public transportation, car pool; buy grocery items on sale, shop at Trader Joes, farmers markets, Wal-Mart, and Costco; cook simple dinners at home; only buy clothes on sale and/ or from discount stores; ask all your utility companies to lower your bills for your "loyalty." Never buy soft drinks, water, or snacks; instead buy a Britta water filter for your home, and for snacks eat only nuts. Live by your needs, not by your wants. A money saver needs to be thrifty with money and know how to calculate earned interest on his or her money.

Warning

A money saver should always check his earned interest by using the formulas below. Some banks are simply fleecing their customers by giving them less in earned interest. It has happened to me many times.

Usually when I confronted a bank manager about it, he was arrogant: "You are the only person who noticed and complained." Interpretation: Sadly millions of bank customers never checked their earned interest to find out if it was calculated correctly. Banks know it and pray on the unsuspecting. This bank was robbing each customer of $50–$450, and from 1 million customers, stealing a total of $50–$450 million annually and getting rich.

The same warnings apply to borrowers. It is recommended they should always check the amount of interest they pay on their loans, mortgages, and credit cards. The same could happen here; lenders can inflate actual interest rates/amounts and borrowers can end up overpaying their loans without knowing it.

Example #1: CDs accounts.
Formula—how to calculate earned interest

Given: CD account: On July 15, 2014, Robert deposited $67,500 at 5% APY for 12 months.

Find: How much interest did his account earn in 12 months?

There are 2 methods to calculate earned interest in accounts, (1) by memorizing a formula; or (2) by visualizing the equation using common sense, below.

For the 1st method, you need to memorize the formula:
$X = (P \times R) \div 100\%$.

Where:

X — unknown earned interest, in dollars; must find amount

P — principal, in dollars

R — rate of interest, in %

100% — constant coefficient, principal always = 100%

Answer to the above example is:
$X = P \times R \div 100\% = (\$67,500 \times 5\%) \div 100\% = \$3,375$.
Robert earned $3,375 in interest in 12 months.

For the 2nd option, there is no need to memorize the formula; instead, use common sense and visualization:

Formula: $67,500 = 100\%$;

$X = (\$67,500 \times 5\%) \div 100\% = \$3,375$.

$\$X = 5\%$

Where:

$67,500 — principal

100% — principal always assumed to be 100%

5% — interest rate in CDs

X — unknown earned interest; must find amount

$ — money symbols, should lined up in the same vertical raw

% — percentages, should line up in the same vertical raw

Answer is: Robert earned $3,375 in interest.

Example #2: Money market accounts. How to calculate earned interest

Given: Money market account: On May 1, 2014, Robert deposited $35,000 at 4% for 3 months or 90 days.

Find: How much interest did this account earn in 3 months, or 90 days?

a) How much interest did this account earn in 12 months, or 365 days?

Answer: $35,000 = 100%;

X = ($35,000 x 4%) ÷ 100% = $1,400 in 365 days;

$X = 4%

b) How much interest did this account earn in 90 days?

Answer: $1,400 = 365 days;

X = ($1,400 x 90 days) ÷ 365 days = $345.20

X = 90 days

Where:

$35,000 — principal

100% — principal always assumed to be 100%

4% — interest rate in CDs

365 days — days in 12 month

90 days — money deposited for 90 days

X — unknown earned interest; must find amount

$ — money symbols, should lined up in the same vertical raw

% — percentages, should line up in the same vertical raw

Answer: This money market account earned $345.20 in 90 days.

Rule of 72, Another Formula for Savers

Rule of 72 is a quick approximate way to find out how long it will take to double your money at a given compound interest rate.

Example

How long will it take to double money from $10,000 to $20,000 at a 5% compound rate?

Rule of 72 formula: $T = 72 \div R = 72 \div 5 = 14.4$ years. Answer: It will take 14.4 years to double money.

<u>Where:</u>

T — Time in years

72 — constant, coefficient

R — rate, compound interest rate

○ ○ ○

THE MORAL OF THE STORY

Become a powerful person: Learn to save, put savings into CDs and money market accounts, and earn interest on it. It is true that "Money does grow on trees"—when people become money savers. Money grows from interest rates without you working for it.

Saving money is a skill that makes savers creative and powerful. It increases their self-esteem and helps keep their life under their control. That is why and how interest rate was the greatest invention of the 19th century.

When on the other hand, savers cannot control other people, such as Wall Street fund managers, mortgage bankers and credit card lenders; other people and their actions are beyond the saver's control.

Always remember this wise saying: "It is better to have one bird in your hands than hundreds of birds in the sky." Interpretation: It is better to have money in your saving accounts that is increasing and under your control than to give your hard-earned money to other people to gamble (i.e., the Wall Street fund managers and various financial advisors). Learn to respect money.

Keep saving money every day, as it is a very powerful tool that is under your control. From the above examples learn about the very important formulas that shows how to calculate earned interest, and use it every day!

SHORT STORY

#**6**

How to Cure Headaches, Migraines, Peripheral Neuropathy, and Fibromyalgia

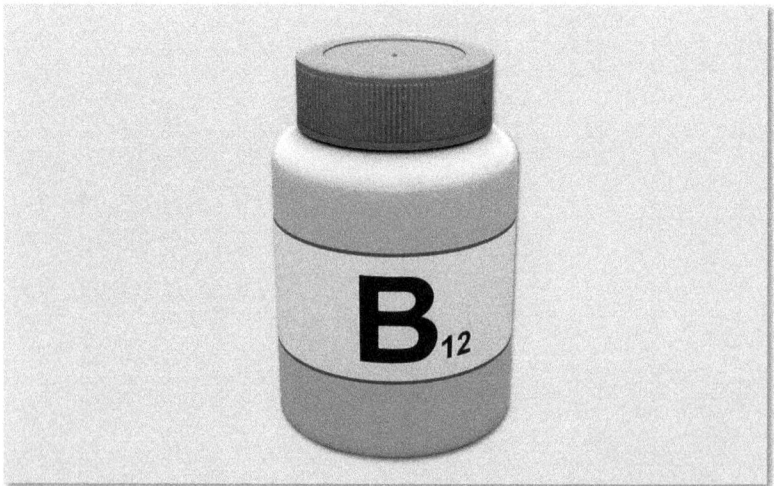

o   o   o

A Case of Rheumatoid Arthritis?

I arrived in Tampa, Florida, to get some sun and to cure myself from the ill side effects of osteoporosis drugs. To me the sun was life!

At the same time, I had a 2nd set of health problems that the sun could not cure completely. My wrists were swollen, especially the right one that I used to hold a computer mouse. My hands and fingers were in spasms and tingling with hundreds of sharp needles; the same thing in my feet and toes.

With those symptoms, I went to see several physicians, all of whom gave the same diagnosis: "You have rheumatoid arthritis and should take medication." I was prescribed 4 different medications. I was skeptical and strongly believed that I did not have rheumatoid arthritis. I had no reason to have it. However, I tried 2 out of the 4 prescribed drugs and 2–3 days later, the 1st side effect appeared—double vision. Alarmed, I stopped driving and stopped taking these drugs.

My health problems intensified, and I kept looking for a physician who could help me. Finally I found one who agreed with me that I did not have rheumatoid arthritis. I trusted him. What I had, he said, was peripheral neuropathy and fibromyalgia. He sent me for physical therapy where an electrical current, as a stimulator, was applied to my hands and feet. After 2 weeks of treatment, there was no improvement, and I quit this therapy.

Then, the physician decided to give me an injection of vitamin B. I fainted. During the commotion, another physician from the next room came to see what had happened. On his notepad he wrote: "Go to Walgreens [pharmacy] and buy the sublingual vitamin B complex with B12, and use it under your tongue every morning."

Vitamin B Complex and B12

Without any hesitation, I started taking the vitamin B complex with B12. In approximately 2–3 weeks, my 2nd set of illnesses entirely disappeared. I was not having painful wrist swellings, no pins and needles or tingling in my hands and feet. The rheumatoid arthritis, peripheral neuropathy, and fibromyalgia all disappeared. Unexplained and for good!

As our body ages, it starts to malfunction and we naturally succumb to greater maladies. The production by our bodies of vitamins and minerals also decreases, which I learned about it from internet health websites.

For instance, by age 40, the production of vitamin B and B12 in our bodies drops to 50%. The lack of those vitamins, such as in my case, led to peripheral neuropathy and fibromyalgia. In addition, many people, due to lack of B12, develop headaches and migraines.

Stabbing Headaches

Recently, 1 year ago, out of the blue, I started having stabbing headaches. They came suddenly, and randomly, and attacked the front of my head in a cluster of 8–10 stabs. Each stab lasted less than a fraction of a second. Then, stabs disappeared as suddenly as they had come.

What was it? Was it real or was it just my imagination? It was a frightening feeling. I searched the internet and found many community and forums where there were discussions about the same symptoms, stabbing headaches. On these sites, there were many questions and suggestions about what to do.

I went to a neurologist. He was not helpful, saying: "Oh, I am very much familiar with your stabbing headaches. One of my patients had this kind and committed suicide." He sent me to get an MRI. I went to another neurologist. He referred me to a pain management clinic for injections in the back of my head.

I scanned the internet about the pain relief injections into the back of the head and found that they were dangerous. No one knows the potential side effects; how the brain could react to injected drugs; plus the injections gave only temporary relief. At the same time, they could trigger many other symptoms, including high blood pressure. Injected drugs could create a shock to the brain, reacting with the brain's substances and producing new brain illnesses.

It is a fact that some patients who undergo heart surgery and are injected with a huge amount of anesthesia, later committed suicide. I thought it was a very risky adventure for me.

Now I knew that injected drugs could cause considerable harm to my brain and probably would produce additional brain symptoms or illness.

What Triggered My Stabbing Headaches?

That evening, I went to bed early to process and sort out the information I had received and try to find a solution to my stabbing headaches. I started processing information using one of the laws of life that was very familiar to me: "Nothing happens by accident; there must be a reason for it." Indeed, why suddenly, out of the blue, had I started having stabbing headaches?

I took an inventory of my headaches of the past. As long as I could remember, I never suffered from headaches or migraines, as some of my friends did. In the past, sometimes I had tension headaches.

They were during school exams, when I studied for many hours and my mind endured great stress. Once

I passed the exams, the stress disappeared and so did my headaches. Or, during my working life, for many days when I was under stress.

I also took stock of my life activities in the last month. What had I done differently in the last month versus before? What did I eat? Was my food different? What new activities had I undertaken now versus before? What triggered those stabbing headaches?

Trigger and the Cure for the Stabbing Headaches

Soon I found both, the problem and the solution. You see, approximately 3–4 weeks before I had developed the headaches, I had seen on the news that vitamins were toxic, and many of them have side effects.

I had decided to take a break from the vitamins I had been taking for years—and when the stabbing headaches had arrived.

Knowing how vitamin B and B12 was important for the brain and body to function, I resumed taking vitamin B complex with B12 and the rest of the vitamins that I had taken regularly before.

In a few days, the frequency of the stabbing headaches diminished and 1 week later they disappeared for good.

As of today, I continue taking sublingual vitamin B complex with B12 every morning.

○ ○ ○

THE MORAL OF THE STORY

The most important #2 vitamins in the body are vitamin B complex and B12, especially for the brain and the nervous system. A lack of it triggered headaches, migraines, peripheral neuropathy, and fibromyalgia. I learned that from information from the internet, my personal experience, and some doctors' shows, and health websites.

The #1 most important vitamin in the body is vitamin D. The sun produces vitamin D when its rays come into the body through the corner of the eyes.

Please see my other short story in the trilogy titled "Why Africans have less heart diseases, diabetes, and cancer? And no depression, osteoporosis, arthritis, or asthma?"

"Nothing happened by an accident, there is always a reason for it," please read the following story #7. Always analyze the problem, find the reason and create a solution for it.

Remember the greatest wealth you have—is your health.

SHORT STORY

#7

Nothing Happens by Accident. There Is Always a Reason for It

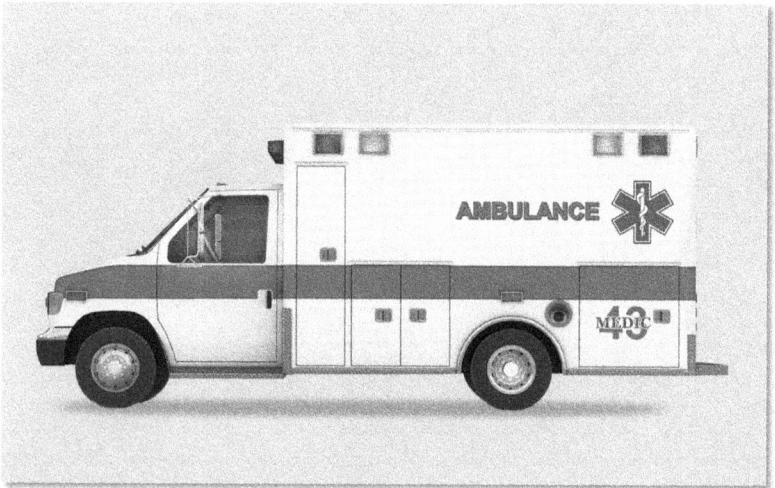

○ ○ ○

"Nothing happens by accident, there is always a reason for it."

My grandmother Anna

A Life-Threatening Event

I woke up in the middle of the night in a fright—something terrible was happening to me. My heart was bursting with pain. "Am I having a heart attack?" I thought. The nausea, sweat, and dizziness were overwhelming. I reached for the phone to call 911. I was fainting. "How will an ambulance reach me? By breaking down the doors?" the next thoughts zipped across my mind, as I was living in a big apartment complex.

I went into survival mode. I grabbed a coat and ran outside to the street, thinking that if I fainted, at least someone would find me there on the street. I remembered that across the street, there was a CVS pharmacy open 24 hours. I headed in that direction. Frightened, my mind was on fire, searching for information in the deep folds of my brain on how to save myself.

Memories of my childhood flashed across my mind, from when my grandma Anna often had episodes of high blood pressure late at night. She would wake me up and say, "Alla, Alla call an ambulance for grandma!" I would call them and wait on the street to show them which apartment we lived in, since we lived in a big metropolitan city.

The Russian ambulances were equipped with 2 physicians who were specialists in emergency situations. That way, they could help a patient immediately on the premises without bringing the majority of them into the hospital emergency room.

The physicians would immediately examine grandma. Once they found that she had high blood pressure, they would give her a nitroglycerin tablet under her tongue. Then, they would wait for 20–30 minutes, checking her vital signs and the direction of her blood pressure. They would give her a 2nd nitroglycerin tablet if her blood pressure rose again. Once they were sure they had stabilized grandma, and she was out of danger, they left. During these dire events I, as a child, would watch what occurred intensely and cry thinking that grandma was going to die.

When I reached the pharmacy and told the pharmacist that I was having a heart attack, she took my blood pressure. It was 247/112 mm Hg. I was going to die, or have a heart attack. I know that an ambulance was like a taxi, by the time I reached the help in the hospital, it probably would be too late.

I asked the pharmacist to give me a nitroglycerin tablet. She called my physician. Luckily, someone was on duty and immediately prescribed me nitroglycerin. I took the 1st tablet and 5 minutes later the 2nd tablet. My blood pressure quickly went down to 200/96 mm hg, then 20–30 minutes later went up again, like a yoyo. That was how, starting from this 1st episode, that this life-threatening event kept repeating for the next 5–6 weeks.

Before that, all my life I had low blood pressure; in fact, I was probably born with that way. Every morning, as soon as I woke up and started moving, I would get dizzy, all because my blood pressure was low. To raise my blood pressure, I would drink a cup of coffee. Later in life, I started having orthostatic hypotension where my blood pressure became even lower.

I questioned: what was happening now? Why had my low, orthostatic hypotension suddenly, in just one night, reversed 180 degrees in the opposite direction? From one extreme (low) to another extreme (high)? Almost every night, I started having extremely high blood pressure, sweating, nausea, and dizziness, all accompanied by fainting.

Why? What had happened? It did not happen by accident. There was a reason for it—a trigger had to be responsible for it! But what was the trigger?

I had been in the emergency room in the local hospital and in the university hospital many times. Physicians had no clue why it was only late at night that my blood pressure suddenly rose to an extremely high level for several hours, like a tornado. During these episodes I was taking nitroglycerin tablets that were making my blood pressure zigzag up and down. Then, by late morning, the tornadoes disappeared, and my blood pressure spiraled down. During the day it was normal, regardless of my activities or emotions.

In the hospital[1] I was usually hooked up to a blood pressure monitor. At night, when I was sleeping, the nurse would wake me up, warn me that my blood pressure was very high, and give me nitroglycerine tablets. Very often during these episodes of high blood pressure, I also fainted.

My life was a nightmare and I saw no light at the end of the tunnel. But what was my diagnosis? Some physicians said nothing. Others gave me a diagnosis like: "You are Russian, and that is why your blood pressure is extremely high at night, and during the day it is normal." To them, the 11-hour time zone difference between Moscow and California was the reason, and me being a Russian meant my body was running on Moscow time.

Usually patients have high blood pressure during the day from certain events, stresses, or emotions and not during the night when they are sleeping, as was the case with me. I protested, stating that such a "diagnosis" was nonsense.[2]

I had been in the USA for a long time, and I was sure my body had had plenty of time to adjust to the time zone differences during that period. I kept repeating this to the physicians and staff and anyone who was willing to listen to my law of life: "Nothing happens by accident, there is a reason for my high blood pressure." But what was it?

Something dramatic was happening in my body late at night that was triggering these life-threatening bouts of high blood pressure. But what? What was the trigger? The physicians had yet to find out.

In hospitals, staff always took my EKGs, and they were normal. So the physicians blamed me, the patient, saying, "Your EKG is normal. You have nothing!" As if an EKG was a correct test for diagnosing my symptoms. I did not accept it and challenged them with undisputable facts. I reminded them about the fact that the majority of patients who died from heart attacks had normal EKGs.

I cited the classic example of President Bill Clinton. All his medical tests were normal. At the same time, he was dying from heart disease, as his arteries were 90% blocked.

President Clinton's Medical Record

President Clinton's medical record is a classic example of incorrect medical tests. The fact was, President Clinton almost died from a heart attack and underwent quadruple bypasses surgery because his arteries were 90% blocked.

How long did it take to clog his arteries by 90%? One month? One year? No, it took 10–15 years. During a portion of those 10–15 years, 1992–2000, he was the President of the USA.

He had a 24/7 team of supposedly "the best physicians in the USA." Every year he took a thorough physical exam and also many high advanced medical tests at Bethesda Naval Hospital, Maryland. All his exams and tests were normal. And year after year, his medical teams announced to the American people that President Clinton had a "clean bill of health".

They even screwed up his quadruple bypass heart operation.[3] After this operation, he aged by 20 years and started dying. Concerned newsrooms and the public saw him on TV looking frail and ghostly, something was wrong with President Clinton. Then, "the best thoracic surgeons" took him back and repeated the heart operation for the 2nd time.

They poured pints of anesthetic drugs into his body during his 2 heart operations. Those drugs will stay in his body for the rest of his life, reacting with all the substances inside his body and damaging his internal organs, especially his brain and liver. It was not by accident that after 2 such major operations he started acting strange for several months. (The fact is, among all operations, the highest number of patients who commit suicide shortly after the operation are open heart surgery patients.)

As for President Clinton's heart illness, his lifestyle played an important part in it. Why and how? It was a well-known fact that President Clinton liked junk food or fast food. For most of his life, he ate it almost every day. TV cameras often showed him jogging near the White House and then, at the end of his jog, he would jog directly to McDonald's to get his favorite treat, a Big Mac.

One did not need to be a rocket scientist or rely on medical tests to arrive at this conclusion. Where did all the grease and cholesterol go? Directly to his arteries, as deposits on the wall of his arteries. Physicians don't like to hear such facts and, behind my back, were ridiculing me.

Prepared for My Cremation

My 5–6 weeks of medical crisis also took a toll on my son and his family. They were exhausted, they barely slept, and their nights were preoccupied with me and my health emergencies. My grandchildren would ask me, "Grandma, are you going to die?" I prepared for my cremation. The reality was not if I was going to die, but when.

Then my eldest son insisted that I call his dad, Chrys, my ex-husband, a cardiologist in Baltimore, Maryland (we had been married for 29 years), and in just a minute he saved my life.

Chrys said: "You have secondary hypertension; one of your organs has failed and produced this extreme blood pressure. It could be an adrenalin gland, liver, kidney, heart, thyroid, or any other organ. About 15% of my patients have secondary hypertension. The physicians should put you on Norvask /Amlodipine immediately; that is the only drug I know of that will lower your high blood pressure. They should admit you to the hospital and find out which organ has failed."

I typed out his recommendations, and, after I fainted the next night, went to the emergency room and gave my ex-husband's recommendation to the admitting physician. I was admitted and for 3 days they checked my organs by running complex tests. All the tests were normal.

However, no one checked my thyroid gland. To put hands on my thyroid was a simple, free 1 minute examination and not an expensive test, so no one was interested in checking it. My extreme high blood pressure and fainting events continued.

The Trigger of My Extreme Blood Pressure and Fainting

One day I was watching *The Doctor Oz show*. He suggested that his audience follow his instructions to check their thyroids and nodules. I followed and found that indeed, I had an enlarged thyroid and nodules. My thyroid was the trigger for my sudden illness! My thyroid was malfunctioning. I went on the internet and educated myself about the thyroid.

Later I learned that a healthy thyroid constantly releases hormones into the body, hormones that the body needs to survive and function. When the thyroid gland starts to malfunction, it stops periodic release of hormones into the body. Instead, it starts accumulating them for hours.

Then when the thyroid is saturated from these hormones, it bursts and releases all the hormones into the body at once. The body's system goes into shock, trying to process this huge volume of hormones and blood pressure skyrockets and the heart has to work hard. The process lasts several hours, until all the hormones are processed. Then the body recovers from the shock and the blood pressure returns to normal until the next release, as in my case.

I also started going to endocrinologists to ask for help. One prescribed 5 different hormones. Again, I went on the internet to find out about their side effects and effectiveness. All the drugs had severe side effects.

I asked a 2nd endocrinologist to give me a reference for a blood test, called PTH, to also check my parathyroid (4 small glands). He refused, saying that he was not familiar with the PTH test and was not going to order it. I went to the next and he was familiar with this test. My PTH was high, and my parathyroid were also malfunctioning, according to this test.

I Saw Many More Physicians Outside the Hospitals

Previously, I sought little treatment from physicians; I had never had any serious illnesses that required the aid of a doctor. My children and I had never been seriously sick before. I did not depend on physicians until my 50s, when I started taking drugs for osteoporosis. I had heard a lot of complaints about physicians, 1st from my grandma Anna and then later from my friends.

My grandma liked to go to the medical clinics where the physicians gave her preferential treatment. But when someone would ask her how her visit was, her answers were always the same: "Oh, I wasted my time. They did not even know 5% of what I knew." Hearing that and still being young, I thought that my grandma was bashing the physicians.

Then when I became an adult, I heard similar, or worse comments about physicians from my friends. During those times, I thought something was wrong with my friends, and wondered why they were all bashing physicians.

I met my best friend, Paula, through my then husband, a physician. Paula's young daughter Cindy had hepatitis C, a diagnosis Paula had given her daughter. The physicians she met had stated that Cindy had nothing. Paula took her child to the best physicians, money could buy. They called Paula "a neurotic mother who imagined things." Paula was desperate.

Then one day, she had a breakthrough. She brought Cindy to an emergency room where Chrys was on duty. He had been taking his internship in that hospital and not only did he agree 100% with Paula, he told her that Cindy's hepatitis C was at the last stage. Today or tomorrow, her eyes were going to turn yellow.

He admitted her to the hospital. Paula was so relieved and happy that she kissed Chrys' hand. Imagine the desperation the mother was going through all that time. Cindy recovered and Paula was like a tick after Chrys; she did not want to lose him. She had a party and invited Chrys and I, and our small children. From that time, she became my best friend, my sister, and my mother.

Unfortunately, many years later, I became sick and it was my time to have bad experiences with physicians, as my grandma and my friends had before me. I knew well that health care was an art, not engineering. Just go to 5 different physicians, and you will get 5 different diagnoses.

For my high blood pressure, besides hospitals, I went to see many more physicians. No one had any idea what was going on with me. No one cared; no one made any effort to accurately diagnose or attempt to pinpoint what was triggering my high blood pressure. To justify their charges for a "consultation," they usually uttered one short sentence that made no sense, or had little relevance to my condition.

Usually I came to these consultations, or visits, with a short summary or status of my illness, typed on 1 page. On the 2nd page was a graph from the university hospital stay showing how my blood pressure had been fluctuating during a 24-hour period. Those 2 pages described my illness in simple form, so even a child could understand it.

It took less than 5 minutes to scan those 2 pages. Please judge the physicians that I saw for yourself from some of my examples below.

Example #1

After scanning the 2 pages of my health status, a physician asked a few unimportant questions. At the end he said, "Oh, well, when you come the next week for the follow up visit, I will give you some drugs to try." Then, he gave me a form he had marked showing that I had a "consultation" with him that day, and scheduled the follow-up appointment in a week.

I gave his form to his receptionist and refused to schedule the follow-up visit.

The receptionist said, "You must schedule the next visit; you are assigned to this doctor." I left. In 2–3 days, I received a telephone call from her insisting the same thing: "You are assigned to this doctor. Your appointment was scheduled on....(she gave me a date)."

Again, I refused, and faxed a letter to this physician informing him that he had no business "to assign me to him." It was my health and my money, and I would go to any physician I liked. I had no obligation to go to him only.

To my disbelief, I soon learned that being "assigned to a physician" was almost the norm in California. In California, physicians had created some kind of oligopoly, a group of say, 5–10 of them with the same specialty, in the same office, made their own laws and regulations.

Once a patient saw their 1st physician in such a group, he was automatically "assigned to him." The patient could not switch to another physician in the same group. Their inside law did not allow this and the patient had no other alternative.

All the physicians in that town with the same specialty had grouped together. To see another physician in this specialty, a patient would have to travel to another town.

Example #2

Another physician gave his assessment of my health: "Oh, today your blood pressure is high, but the next week when you come in, it will probably be lower." What kind of nonsense was that?

Fact is: blood pressure is changing every minute, as much as 10–30 points, lets alone in weeks. That was the typical pattern. My appointment was at 9 a.m.; my blood pressure was 170–180 mm hg. It dropped from 220–230 mm hg at night. By 10 a.m. or 11 a.m., it would usually become normal until late at night when it spiked again. In front of her was the diagram of how my blood pressure had been fluctuating during a 24-hour period.

Example #3

At the end of my visit, I asked the physician: "What can you do for me?" He replied: "What can I do for you? You blood pressure is normal." I said nothing; it was useless.

My appointment with him was at 3 p.m. and of course, my blood pressure during this time of the day was always normal as was clearly indicated on my blood pressure diagram that I gave to him as soon as I entered his room. *The fact is that blood pressure is fluctuating every minute as much as 20–30 points, and fluctuates more so in any given day.*

Example #4

After reading 2 pages of my health status, this physician lashed out at me: "I consider this an insult. There is no such thing as secondary hypertension. Everything is secondary." I did not answer; there was no need for me to get confrontational. It was obvious she had no clue. If she visited the internet and typed "hypertension" she would learn that there are 2 types of hypertension: primary and secondary.

Primary hypertension, which 85% of patients have comes from lifestyle choices, stress, or obesity. Secondary hypertension was always triggered by organ failure: i.e., the adrenalin gland, thyroid, liver, kidney, heart, or from snoring. About 15% of patients in Europe had secondary hypertension and 20% in Japan.

In the USA, few patients have been diagnosed with secondary hypertension because not many USA physicians know that there is such an illness as secondary hypertension.

Example #5

I also went to some consultants/experts. They did not accept health insurances. Instead, a patient had to pay cash. I paid $1,200 for the 1st consultation, then $600 for follow-up visits. His recommendation was: "Stop, stop taking the Amlodipine drug!" I asked him: "Then what drug should I take instead?" Him: "When you come next week, I will tell you." I left.

My son was angry at me: "You behave like a little mouse. Why didn't you ask him what you should take instead?" "I asked him, but he did not answer," I said. Of course I erred on the side of caution. I did not stop taking Amlodipine. The next week, during the follow-up visit, I asked this expert-consultant 2 times, what should I take instead of Amlodipine? He kept silent; he did not answer. I stopped going to him.

Example #6

I tried another expert/consultant. Again, I paid him $1,000 in cash. At the end of the consultation, I asked him what he thought I had. He answered: "You have celiac disease." Me: "What is that?" He did not answer.

I asked him to write the name of this disease on a piece of paper, so I would not forget it. He wrote on his notepad: celiac disease. I came home and Googled it.

The answer was that it was a stomach disease and a major symptom of it was diarrhea. I hit the ceiling. I did not have celiac disease. And even if I did have it, I did not care; it was not a life-threatening disease—but my extreme high blood pressure was.

I had gone to him to find out what was triggering my extreme blood pressure. I was not looking for some fabricated, exotic disease. Having no clue how to help me, he invented the exotic celiac disease just to divert attention from my real health problem to something imaginary. I did not go back to him for a follow up visit. Instead, I faxed him my above analysis of my consultation with him.

Summary

During all this time, I spent many times in hospital emergency rooms, or days when admitted to hospitals; looking for and seeing many physicians for help; but my extreme blood pressure was not dormant as I was waiting for a diagnosis.

It was destroying my heart and tearing up my arteries. I developed angina, then atrial fibrillation that left my left atrium extremely enlarged. My heart became very weak and sick. It could not pump blood efficiently. Then, having no strength, it would beat much quicker and harder, palpitating over 110 beats/min at rest and 150–180 beats/min when walking or after any kind of exertion; I developed atrial fibrillation.

○ ○ ○

THE MORAL OF THE STORY

Nothing happens by accident. There are always reasons for that. Life gives us challenges to teach us lessons, and get new skills. As the patient, I helped myself. It seemed no one wanted me to recover.

If I were a passive patient, I would not be writing this book. I would not be recounting the loss of my health. I got nothing from hospital emergency rooms, or from outside physicians, and cash-only "consultants." Except, I almost died (it was my ex-husband who saved my life), and I wasted my time and money. I spent hundreds of thousands of dollars, and I was frightened, stressed, frustrated, sick, and disappointed.

In the meantime my extreme high blood pressure was not staying dormant waiting for the hospitals and physicians to figure out my diagnosis and help me. Instead, it kept destroying my heart and tearing up my arteries. Medicine is an art, not a science or engineering. Just go to 3–4 physicians, and you will get 3–4 different diagnoses.

Unfortunately the USA is the only country in the world where health care is a private business, where 70% of operations are not necessary and physicians are rich.

In the rest of the world, health care is free for every citizen and the majority of physicians are women.

Physicians are assigned to places where there is a need for them, not where they want to work. Even more, the quality of health care in the USA is behind all developed nations. Americans live 6 years shorter than Europeans, and at the end of their lives almost all finish living in nursing homes.

Your health—is your greatest wealth.

[1]   How many patients die from medical mistakes in the USA hospitals? Between 210,000 — 440,000 patients each year, as per the Journal of Patient Safety. In any given year hospital care contributed to the death of 180,000 patients on Medicare alone, as per The Office of the Inspector General for the Department of Health and Human Services. Medical mistakes are the 3rd leading cause of death in the USA (#1 heart disease, #2 cancer.)

[2]   1 in 20 adults, or 12 million patients a year who seek medical care in the USA are misdiagnosed, according to the journal of BMJ Quality and Safety, published on April 16, 2014. These are patients with conditions as varied as heart failure, pneumonia, anemia, lung cancer, etc.

[3]   The research analyses published on December 19, 2012 in the journal Surgery, used malpractice records to find major surgical errors. It concluded that between 1990 and 2010 more than 80,000 major surgical errors happened.In "US health report card: 'A' for spending, 'F' for performance," "the United State health-care system has finished dead last – yet again- in comparison of first-world countries, despite vastly outspending those nations on health services." Report published by CNBC's Dan Mangan, Health Care Reporter on June 16, 2014 where the USA average spending on health care per capita $8,508 versus UK $3,182, Canada $4,522.

The same time, AMA, spent millions every year to brainwash and program the population. That "our health care is the best in the world; we have scientific breakthrough, etc." Fact is: the USA health care is the worst amount all developed countries, #36.

Americans live 6 years shorter than Europeans and majority of them in the end would finished living in nursing homes.

8

SHORT STORY

Look at the Messenger: Who Is He? Whose Interest Is He Pursuing?

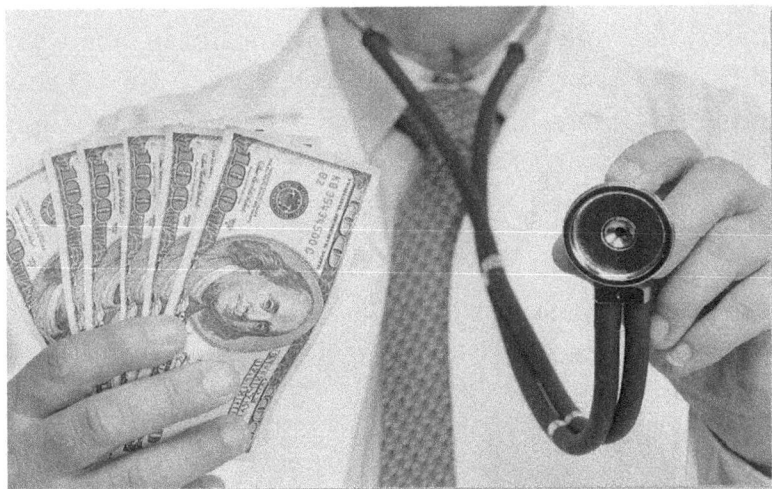

○ ○ ○

When I was a young child, sometimes I would come home very disappointed, complaining about the bad acts and misbehavior of some adults. My grandmother Anna reassured me that I should not get disappointed with strangers. Instead, I should ask myself a question: who are those people? Whose interests are they defending or pursuing? They were not one of my family, relatives or friends or teachers. They did not care about my feelings or interests.

My grandmother was teaching me some life skills. Not to judge people from myself, and not to expect that everyone acted and reacted as I expected them to behave.

Later, as I was growing up, I learned that people were different. Everyone has the baggage of their accumulated information, knowledge, experiences, and beliefs. I learned I should analyze people's intentions, using common sense, logic, and draw my own conclusions.

For the 1st part of my life as an adult, I was lucky. Even if I met some "messengers" or scam artists, I did not have much need for their services, or I probably did not recognize their true intentions, so I suspected nothing.

In this short story, I am not going to recite all the examples of my experiences with those who were scamming me for my money. Here I am going to introduce only 2 such examples, about physicians who took advantage of my vulnerable health situation and my youth, with an intention to harm my health, or my life. I never expected or imagined such a thing could happen to me.

A Trap

One day, suddenly, out of the blue, my heart started palpitating violently. I checked my pulse rate on a blood pressure monitor and it was 110-130 beats/min at rest. First, I thought that as suddenly as it started, it would stop the same way. I waited for 4 days, but my palpitations continued.

I went to see a cardiologist. He ordered an EKG and 48-hour monitor and both showed that I had an atrial fibrillation (heart palpitations and a high heart rate). Later, he sent me to a specialist, a physiologist.

In the morning, before my 2:00 p.m. appointment with the physiologist, his office called asking to see me at 11:00 a.m. between his surgeries, in the hospital. I thought nothing of it, and went to the hospital. He met me in his full surgical garb in the surgery department and escorted me to a conference room. I raised my eyebrows. He had paraded across the hospital picking up germs and bacteria to infect the patient in his operating room![1]

As usual, I gave him a 2-page typed status of my heart aliment so he would be clearly informed. Instead of showing any interest in my illness and asking me questions about it, he got straight to his business and started marketing his service, a cardioversion. (Cardioversion procedures deliver an electric shock to the heart.)

"You see," he started, "for cardioversion, you must take a risk. Everything is a risk. I can do your cardioversion very quickly in the next 2 days."

Ahead of my visit with him, I had already educated myself about atrial fibrillation, (Afib for short) from the internet and the latest "Management of A Fib" book written by a qualified PhD expert and a physician from the Johns Hopkins University.

Next, he directed me to his office to fill out some forms as a new patient. In his office, his staff gave me several forms to sign. All the forms were designed to protect him and ensure he would not be held liable for any terrible outcome from my cardioversion.

As for the form about the status of my health, there was none. Instead, they gave me one form in which to fill in my demographics, insurance details, who was responsible for my medical bills, and whom to contact in case of an emergency.

In the past, I had seen many physicians and they all had health forms asking many questions about the patient's health status and symptoms. This physiologist had none. Driving home, I stewed over my appointment with him and it raised many red flags.

I started asking myself, whose interest was he pursuing? His or mine?

Whose Interest Is the Messenger Pursuing?

I had already learned that a cardioversion[2] was performed only after a patient's blood was 2 times thinner than it should be. Before a cardioversion, a patient was usually put on blood thinning medication for 3–4 weeks; a typical drug used to do that was Coumadin (Coumadin actually is a rat poison). When the blood is thin, a patient has less probability of having blood clots, a stroke, or a heart attack during the electric shock of the heart.

Even more, at least 3–4 weeks before a cardioversion, every 7 days a patient must take a blood test in the lab to monitor the progress of the blood-thinning agent. The patient's blood must be the same consistency during the 3–4 weeks preceding the cardioversion.

The blood test results were crucial. If a patient's blood was too thick, there was risk of a blood clot or stroke. If a patient's blood was too thin, there was a risk the patient could bleed to death.

This physiologist did not prescribe Coumadin for me to take for 3–4 weeks, and he made no reference to taking a lab blood test to monitor my blood consistency 3–4 weeks before cardioversion. Instead, he ordered my cardioversion in a few days. That was a shocking criminal act.

Then, a few days later, I received a telephone call from the hospital. A gentlemen introduced himself and said he was calling on behalf of this physiologist, who had instructed him to register me for the cardioversion procedure. I refused.

Shortly after that, I received a telephone call from my eldest son on the East Coast, yelling, screaming, and accusing me of something. He was very agitated and incomprehensible. When he calmed down, I learned that this physiologist called him informing him that he scheduled a cardioversion for me, but they "…could not locate" me.

My son, knowing my heart status very well, interpreted this to mean I had died. He had looked at his watch to check the time of the day to see if he could catch a direct flight from the East Coast to the West Coast. In distress, on a hunch he dialed my telephone number, thinking that I had left some messages. Instead, I had picked up the phone as cool as a cucumber.

That physiologist continued hunting me as if I was a wounded animal. That was not the end. Then, 2–3 days later his office called, reminding me: "Tomorrow you have a cardioversion scheduled in the hospital." I refused again.

Hunting Me, the Patient

This physiologist saw that I was a vulnerable and sick patient, and my physician had referred me to him to perform a cardioversion. His problem was that this scary procedure was a very short one, taking only 5–10 minutes, and insurance did not pay much for it.

For him, the payment was peanuts, but at the same time he did not want to lose the opportunity to make a lot of money from my illness. He took advantage of me, or: *"Carpe Diem,"* which in Latin stands for *"Seize the Day."* That is how, before I came in, he had already developed an elaborate trap and scam. He scheduled my cardioversion to be carried out in the next few days, skipping the basic 3–4 weeks requirements before the cardioversion.

Why? Very simple. If my blood was thick (as it would be if I took no Coumadin for 3–4 weeks to make my blood thin), I would probably have a life-threatening event: a clot, stroke, or both, or heart attack. And he, to treat such complications, would keep receiving tens of thousands of dollars from my health insurances.

Even more, now he would have an opportunity to perform a very complicated and long operation on my heart, called an ablation.

Ablation is a very serious heart operation. It takes 5–7 hours (much longer than open heart surgery), and after a 1st ablation, a 2nd one must be repeated, since, according to statistics, atrial fibrillation returns in the majority of cases.

Let's not forget that in addition to all the danger and complications associated with such procedures, he would be billing my insurance companies as well. To enrich himself, he was hunting me to destroy my health and my life.

Gynecologist Objective to Cut Out an Organ from My Body

One more example to prove the law of life: "Look at the messenger. Whose interest is he pursuing?"

Many years ago, when I was a young, healthy woman, I went to the gynecologist for just an annual check up; I had no problems. After my examination, he took my hand into his and in a soft voice, his eyes watering, he begged me, "Please, let's do a hysterectomy."

I was terrified. "For what reason?" I asked him bluntly. "You do not need a uterus very much," he replied. The gynecologist's objective was to cut out an important organ from my body.

I told him that in the Soviet Union, a physician would get a 5-year mandatory prison sentence for performing such an operation, and the state would revoke his license. There, to perform a hysterectomy, a physician must obtain permission from the Ministry of Health. Why? Because the uterus plays an important role in a woman's overall health; it produces many hormones. Without uterus, a woman must be put on many hormones medications for the rest of her life to artificially "replace" hormones than her uterus produces. Drugs have many life-threatening side effects and will make her much sicker than before.

I called my best friend Paula about this terrifying visit. She was older, wiser, and had 5 sisters; she knew the gynecologist's reason for the operation: "Of course, he wants to do a hysterectomy[3] on you, to make more money.

"Your annual office visits brings him no money, but your operation will. He will pocket many thousands for this operation and complications after operation. Plus, from now on, you are his patient for life, with several visits per year. For the rest of your life, you will depend on him for giving you hormone drug prescriptions and going back to him for side effects from those drugs." As always, I learned from Paula and stopped going to him.

Summary

The physiologist saw an opportunity to enrich himself at my expense, the patient. Plus, I could do nothing. I had signed several forms absolving him from all consequences. That was why he scheduled my cardioversion a few days later, from the time I saw him the 1st time.

Intentionally, he overlooked the standard 3–4 weeks of blood-thinning procedures and labs, risking that I would have a clot, a stroke, or a heart attack, and he would continue collecting a lot of money from my health insurances.

The same occurred with the gynecologist, entrapping me to cut out a very important organ from female anatomy, the uterus, so I would be sick and became his permanent patient for the rest of my life.

In my case, if I did not realize the physiologist's intention to hurt me, I am sure I would not be writing this story. Or I would have had a clot, a stroke, or heart attack and had 2 or more ablations; and if I survived—then I would have become his patient for life.

o o o

THE MORAL OF THE STORY

Look at the messenger. Whose interest is he pursuing? His interests or yours? Watch for different types of messengers such as: physicians, lawyers, accountants, bankers, mortgage brokers, financial advisors, insurance salesmen, real estate agents, mortgage bankers, car salesmen, or car repair men.

Here, I intentionally selected physicians to emphasize the tragic fact that, physicians to make more money from patients, are willing to perform needless or risky procedures, so they may continue receiving a huge stream of income for complications after the procedures.

Physicians know that an injured patient is a regular patient for life. You, as a patient, have health objectives that are different from that of physicians'. Your objectives are to cure your illnesses and recover.

Physicians' objectives are to get rich from your illnesses and continue getting a stream of income from your illnesses. If a patient is cured and recovers, then the physician's income stops.

Only you, the patient, can help yourself to find a correct diagnosis. Who knows your body better than you do? Medicine is an art, not engineering. It is just common sense. Be responsible for your health and life. Especially now, with all the information you need being available on the internet and TV physicians shows. A physician is not going to search the internet regarding a patient's illness; a patient should do that.

Take care of your health—it is your greatest wealth.

---

[1]   Hospital stays result in over 720,000 infections yearly, according to new data from the Centers for Disease Control and Prevention that highlighted the need to prevent such infections.

[2]   When a physiologist attaches 2 patches to a patient's chest and presses the button for an electric shock to jolt the patient's heart.

[3]   A classic example. Every year over 600,000 hysterectomies are performed in the USA for unwarranted and unnecessary reasons. 1 in 3 women in the USA can expect to have a hysterectomy by the age of 60, the highest percentage in the industrial world. Please see NIH (National Institute of Health), Wikipedia, etc. In Europe, these numbers are much lower.

SHORT STORY

9

Everyone Wants You to Be Stupid. Why? So They Can Make Money from You

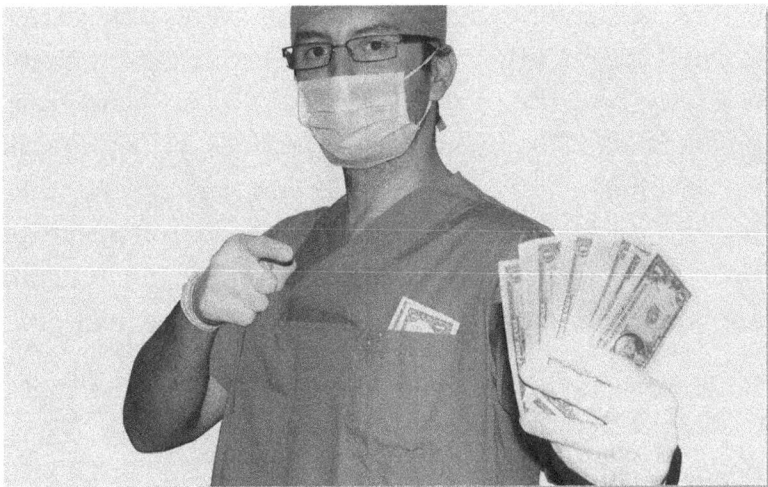

O O O

"Everyone wants you to be stupid, so they can make money from you."

Anonymous

When other people complain to me about the problems they have experienced, some of them wisely finish summarizing their problem-incident with a wise observation or expression: "Everyone wants you to be stupid, so they can make money from you."

All these complaints involved money they paid for services. Here, in this story, I am applying this wise expression to more serious problems involving health and illnesses.

As for services, when physicians were involved, I learned about other types of observations on point from my best friend Paula: "What do you want from physicians? They perform 2 services only: one is prescribing you some dangerous drugs; another is sending you for an operation to cut off some of your anatomy." Those were just words that had no application to me, until I faced my own health crisis.

Suddenly out of the blue in the middle of the night I became very sick, was hospitalized many times, almost died, and saw many physicians.

I was shocked with what I saw and experienced. Besides battling my illness, I was a victim of risky tests, misdiagnosed, received false diagnoses, scheduled for an unneeded operation, and prescribed many medications that had serious side effects.

Now I saw that physicians assumed that I was stupid. To them I could not recognize what was right and what was wrong and, as a lamb, without any resistance, I would allow them to subject my body to needless and risky tests, drugs that have life-threatening side effects, and removing part of my anatomy.

At the beginning I was naive. Then I started "learning by doing" and took matters into my own hands. I began to care about my health and my body and started refusing their unneeded and dangerous services.

I spoke up to defend myself and avoid traps and tricks designed to hurt me. My battle was not a new one. I experienced misdiagnoses before when I was much younger. But that time, I was healthy, did not need physicians, and was going just for some regular checkups. Today my situation was different. I was dangerously sick and badly needed emergency help.

Mammogram Tests

I started getting mammogram tests after age 50. After 3–4 years, during this typical annual test, this test found "something" in my left breast, and I needed a biopsy.

I requested a copy of all my previous breast x-rays, looked at them under the electric lights, compared them with previous years, and saw nothing. I went back to my young gynecologist for his opinion. He sent me directly to a surgeon for a biopsy.[1]

I had an appointment with the surgeon and was shocked by his unprofessionalism. Red flags were everywhere. He did not even have an x-ray film illuminator on the wall to look at my breast x-rays. Instead, he raised my x-ray sheets, aiming them at the electric bulb in the ceiling. He looked routinely at the sheets for just a fraction of a second each and automatically scheduled a biopsy.

Then, to impress me, he brought me into his business executive office furnished with a huge leather chair, executive desk, huge outside window, and some frames on the wall displaying his diplomas.

Compared to his exam room, which was small and had no window. Plus, he did not bother to buy a major and necessary tool, such as an x-ray film illuminator, to look at patients' x-rays; in the exam room he did not bother to examine me.

I did some research about him and found that his specialty was—a rectal surgeon. Why was he performing breast biopsies and breast operations? This was the 2nd red flag. I saw nothing on my breast x-rays; how could they see something in my left breast that I could not? Why had my gynecologist sent me to this rectal surgeon and not to a breast surgeon? I did not trust them.

Then a friend of mine sent me to her physician in the Women's Breast Institute that was conveniently located just across the office from my gynecologist. I saw the director of the center and told her about my concerns. She was very sympathetic, examined me and my x-rays, and found—nothing. She made a comment that my gynecologist had never sent any of his patients to her. Instead, he kept sending all of them to the rectal surgeon.

It was obvious that both my gynecologist and the rectal surgeon were working together in some kind of a joint venture to perform unnecessary operations on women, all to enrich themselves. Otherwise, why didn't my gynecologist send his patients to the Women's Breast Institute, located right next door? I also stopped getting the mammogram tests.

Orthopedics

One day I began having a problem when driving. When I step on the gas pedal, sharp pains would occur on the bottom of my right foot, as if I stepped on a nail.

My friend sent me to her orthopedic surgeon, who was a professor and department chief in the university. His diagnosis was that I had a neuroma. He explained that a nerve was pinched between my 2 toes on my foot, and I need an operation to relieve the nerve.

I trusted him and agreed to have an operation, except I did not want general anesthesia, only a local. The professor never did such operations before under local anesthesia, but upon seeing my persistence, agreed.

Then, he invited his entire class to watch how he was performing an operation when a patient was "alive" and was not put "to sleep." After a few weeks recovery, I stepped on the gas pedal, and again, it felt as if I had stepped on a nail.

The operation was a fiasco. I could not drive and went to another orthopedic surgeon, this time my friend. He told me that indeed I had a neuroma, except it was in another location, parallel to the previous surgery.

Again, I had no alternatives, so I agreed and went through the 2nd operation and recovery. And once I stepped on the gas pedal, it was as if I had again stepped on a nail. The operation had changed nothing, another fiasco.

Hurt and desperate, I took a mirror and started examining the bottom of my foot with my fingers pressing on each area inch by inch. Soon I found the culprit! It was a simple wart embedded into the skin on the bottom of my foot.

Next, I went to a podiatrist to remove this embedded wart. It seemed to me that nothing was easy and simple when dealing with physicians. The podiatrist started playing his game, to get more visits from me and more money for him. He "removed" the wart. When leaving his office, the sharp pains came back. He just scratched the wart's surface and exposed the core. The area became painful as he did not remove it completely.

I turned back and asked him to stop playing games and do a small simple thing and completely remove the embedded wart. I did not need to have 3 appointments with him to remove skin tissue that had an area of 1/8 of an inch. He did what I asked and pains never again returned to my foot.

Endocrinologist Dr. S.

I kept going to Dr. S., an endocrinologist, for follow-up visits. Even he told me that: "I am not familiar with this PTH test and could not order it for you; it is something that I am not familiar with." PTH (parathyroid test) is a routine test in endocrinology. Other endocrinologists were even worse. One prescribed me 4 dangerous hormones, another told me "My way, or the highway."

Then, many months later, during my routine follow-up visit, Dr. S. became very excited, started animatedly asking how I felt (usually he uttered only 2–3 short phrases during my visits) and occupied his time typing some information about me into his computer; 95% of my visit he spent slowly typing.

This time there was no more typing. I was surprised at his deviation from the norm and keenly began watching to see what he was up to. Without any explanation, he called his nurse and in front of me told her to give me an instruction for a thyroid nodules biopsy, and then he left.

I was scared. Without telling me ahead of time or discussing with me what a nodules biopsy entailed, he decided that I should have it before I came for this follow-up visit. He acted as if I was a tool for his self-serving benefit, or he had a supreme power over me, ordering to take out a piece of my anatomy. This was an operation I did not need, did not ask for, nor ever talked to him about.

On the way back home, I was perturbed by his arrogance, complete lack of concern for me, and disrespecting toward me. He was a dangerous physician—it was a trap. Quickly, I started assessing his motives.

Nothing happened by accident; there were reasons for his behavior —I applied this law of life. "Where did he get the information that I have thyroid nodules?" I questioned my memory. Oh, yes, 1 year ago while watching the *Dr. Oz Show* I learned about thyroid nodules. When I examined my neck, I felt something like nodules.

On the next visit to a specialist, I mentioned my findings to him. He did not check if I was correct (never examined my neck), but immediately sent me for an expensive test to screen for nodules. The lab screened and "found" that I indeed had 2 nodules. I was skeptical.[2] Plus, that was not my major problem.

Even if I had it, I could live with it. My major problem was my heart and extreme high blood pressure. So, I ignored this test finding and forgot about it.

But not my endocrinologist, Dr. S. Many months later he, or his nurse, by accident came across my nodules test in my medical history. Excited, he jumped at the opportunity to make big money from a useless and unnecessary nodules operation and complications after operation.

Without 1st discussing it with me if I needed, wanted, or agreed to have this operation, he decided it for me and ordered me to have it. I stopped going to him.

Objectives of European Physicians Versus American Physicians

In Europe health care, as everywhere in the world, is a socialized health care system. It is free to all citizens. European physicians receive a fixed salary from the government, they work in groups learning from each other, and helping each other to find the correct diagnosis and cure for patients. They receive the same salary regardless of how many patients they see, how many operations they performed or how many drugs they prescribed.

That is why European physicians' objectives are to help patients to recover from their illnesses as soon as possible. European physicians have no incentives to make money from their patients' illnesses. They never prescribe routinely dangerous medications, nor do they perform unneeded operations or routinely send patients for dangerous and expensive tests just to make a lot of money for themselves.

Of course, European physicians are not rich or millionaires. European physicians' salaries are low compared to other professions, it is an easy profession, and the majority of physicians are women.

In the USA, health care is private and is very expensive. The USA is the only country in the whole world where health care is private. The majority of Americans cannot afford to pay for this expensive private health care.

That is why the USA government established a social health care system for a part of the population—for seniors and the poor. That is: seniors, from the age of 65 receive Medicare insurance that pays 80% of their Medicare bills; then Medicare recipients must pay the 20% balance from their own pockets.

For poor people, the USA government has Medical Assistance insurance, which is free for the poor. As for the rest of the population? They must find ways to pay for their health care. Some companies pay for their employees' health insurance.

And those companies that do not pay health insurance for their employees? These employees simply have no health insurance, and live on prayers and luck hoping they will be healthy; for example, minimum wage employees, and low salary employees.

American physicians' objectives are just the opposite of European physicians. American physicians' objectives are to make a lot of money from their patients' illnesses. If American patients are not sick, then there are no visits, no prescription drugs, no tests, and no operations. So in this case, what are American physicians going to do? Where will they get money?

That is how and why in the USA, physicians are one of the highest paid professions; they are rich and a lot of them are millionaires. At the same time, American health care quality is the worst and is behind all European countries.

Americans' life expectancy is 6 years shorter versus Europeans', and the majority of Americans end their lives in nursing homes.

Why has such an easy profession, as being a physician, become the most prestigious profession in the USA and the highest paid? (Everywhere in the world majority of physicians are women.)

All because of the marketing and indoctrination by the American Medical Association, AMA, by pharmaceutical companies, and by their army of lobbyists. They spend millions and billions of dollars marketing medical procedures and drugs to USA patients. Then they, the big donors, lobby the Congress, the Senate, and the White House to execute their rackets and schemes.

In the rest of the world, the most prestigious profession is—engineering; their salaries are 2–3 times higher than physicians. Every school child wants to be an engineer and the best are going into engineering universities. Not in the USA—here every child wants to be rich or famous. Or, to be lawyers and physicians.

Who Developed Medical Technology?

All medical technologies are invented, designed, and manufactured—by engineers, not by physicians. MDs (Medical Doctors) are not inventors; they do not design any medical technology.

To create any medical technology requires a special set of skills and knowledge: creativity, problem solving skill, math, physics, and strength of materials; not skills in prescribing drugs or cutting patients bodies with knives.

In short, every device, machine, or test physicians use in their offices, hospital, medical center, and in operating rooms are all designed by engineers. For example: x-ray machines, CT scanners, lasers, pacemakers, stress machines, blood pressure monitors, hearing aids, pacemakers, operating room equipment, transplant equipment, stethoscopes, and thousands more.

In the USA, patients confuse the term of MD with PhD, where MD stands for a Medical Doctor. Yet, here for some convenience, the word "medical" was dropped, and only the word "doctor" is used. So, patients called a medical doctor—just a doctor.

PhD stands for Doctor of Philosophy (taken from Latin Philosophiae Doctor); it is the highest degree awarded by a university to someone who has advanced knowledge in his field and publically defended his dissertation research, which in itself is a new innovation and is a contribution to knowledge.

A doctoral candidate must invent a new idea, then this idea he must developed into a research dissertation, often the length of a book—300 pages or more. Hundreds of doctoral candidates enter the PhD program, but after many years, only a small number of them defend dissertations and receive doctoral degrees. To apply to a doctoral program requires a bachelor's and master's degree, first and foremost. So, the requirements for physicians to received a PhD are as above.

Very few physicians have a PhD, and those who were fortunate enough to receive it are working in medical research labs.

Here is the confusion. When the American public hear that "a doctor" has developed this or that technology, or received a Nobel Prize, they mistakenly think that it was an MD. The fact is that it is an engineer with a doctoral degree, a PhD, or a scientist.

Engineers have developed all medical technologies used in healthcare. The same applies to drugs: drugs are developed by chemical engineers; some of them also have a PhD degree.

Summary

Only when I, the patient, took my health problems into my own hands, was I able to solve my problems and save myself from unneeded and dangerous operations. It was just common sense. Who knew more about my body symptoms, the doctor or I?

Medicine is an art and not an engineering. Just go to 5 physicians and you will get 5 different diagnoses and misdiagnoses. Look at physicians as messengers, asking whose interest are they pursuing?

Unfortunately, the USA is the only country in the whole world where medical care is private and physicians make their money from the volume or supply of services they provide to patients. The USA is a capitalist country and here politicians do not want that their big donors—the American Medical Association, physicians, and pharmaceuticals companies—have socialized medicine as all Europeans and the rest of the world do.

To look at physicians and whose interests they are pursuing is just simple common sense. It is a fact that the more services a physician provides, the more money he makes. It is an instinct for survival. It is not in a physician's personal interest for a patient to recover from his illnesses and never again return to see that physician. Then how is the physician going to maintain his expensive life style or become a millionaire?

To prove this point, let's take an analogy: a repair shop versus a physician. When your car needs repair, you brought it to a repair man, and pay for the needed repairs.

Then, when you start driving, your dashboard again lights up in red because your car was not repaired properly. So what do you do?

Go back to the same repair shop, say nothing, and again ask to have your car repaired, you pay the same amount the 2nd time and when you start driving, again your dashboard is red.

This time you are driving to another repair shop, but pay a much higher amount the 3rd time; this repair shop "found" that you need a new engine (your car is only 6 years old) and charges you $8,000 more. Would you agree with this repair shop and, foolishly, would you give him all your money, for not finding the problem with your car on the 1st visit, and continue paying him again and again?

Of course, with a car repairman you would jump to the ceiling if he did not repair your car the 1st time; and you would demand a full refund. Why patients don't do the same with physicians? You see the point.

o o o

THE MORAL OF THE STORY

Everyone wants you to be stupid. Why? So they can make money from you. Here in this story, I intentionally selected health care services to emphasize the tragic facts that even physicians are willing to hurt patients to make money from them. They do so by manufacturing nonexistent diagnoses, performing unnecessary procedures, operations, and expensive tests; and are prescribing many dangerous drugs to receive bonuses from drugs companies.

"Physicians usually perform 2 typical services: one is prescribing you some drugs; another is sending you for surgery to cut off some parts of your anatomy," this is a typical saying of many wise patients. Surgeons perform surgeries on patients with knives and are surrounded by hundreds of medical technology devices (designed by engineers) to help them to do operations more effectively.

Patients are confusing MD—with PhD. When they hear that a "doctor" invented this or that technology, or a doctor received a Nobel Prize, they wrongly assume that it was an MD when actually it was a PhD, an engineer, or a scientist.

"Everyone want you to be stupid, so they can make money from you," the wise saying states.

Once you are sick you lost interest in money and in all physical assets you have—all because the most important wealth you have—your health.

---

[1] 03/17/2015 NBC Nightly News, and the following days many more national news broadcasted that: As many as one in four breast biopsies are incorrectly diagnosed by pathologists, according to a new study." In an article "Breast Biopsies Leave Room for Doubt, study finds" by Denise Grady, March 17, 2014, where Dr. Joann G Elmore said: "It is often thought that getting the biopsy will give definite answers, but our study says maybe it won't."

[2] 1 in 20 adults, or 12 million patients a year, who seek medical care in the USA are misdiagnosed, according to the journal BMJ Quality and Safety, published on April 16, 2014. Patients with conditions as varied as heart failure, pneumonia, anemia, lung cancer, and many more.

SHORT STORY

Comediante or Tragediante?
Laugh or Cry?

o o o

One evening my then husband Chrys asked me: "Do you know how comedy-tragedy was born? When Napoleon slapped Pope Pius VII in the face, asking for a divorce from Josephine." "No," I responded, and fascinatingly started listening to this intriguing story.

Napoleon Bonaparte was born on the island of Corsica, Italy, in a well-to-do family. He was well educated, joined the French army, and for his bravery was promoted in the later stage of the French Revolution. Napoleon liked the idea of the French Revolution and defended and promoted it. He was a French military general and political leader, who became the First Emperor of France. His drive for military expansion changed the world.

As a young officer, he won all his battles under the command of older men. To show his allegiance to France (he was a Corsican) and at the same time become more reliable in the army's eyes, he decided to get married to an older French woman. In 1796, he married a widow of a French general with 2 children, Rose de Beauharnais, a sophisticated woman, prominent in Paris' high society.[1]

Napoleon did not like her name Rose and renamed her Josephine. He was madly in love with her and wrote her many passionate letters from his campaigns. She despised him at first, never traveled with him, and as soon as he was out and preoccupied with his many campaigns, she had numerous extramarital affairs. Once the rumors about her betrayal reached him, he was despondent and stopped loving her. He started having many mistresses; he even had an illegitimate son, Charles Leon, in 1806.

In 1804, Napoleon became the First Emperor of France. His ambition was to conquer many countries in Europe, so Europe would be united under his empire and function under the ideas of the French Revolution. Napoleon's Empire was growing, and pressure was mounting on him to have an heir. He decided to divorce Josephine who could not produce him a heir.

Pope Pius VII had to annul the marriage between Napoleon and Josephine. Herein lay a big problem. For years, Pius VII was Napoleon's enemy. He was anti-French and was constantly at odds about the new rules to govern church-state relations in France.

Both were on a collision course. When Napoleon became Emperor in 1804, he summoned Pius VII to crown him. At the last moment Napoleon took the crown from Pope's hands and put it on his head crowning himself, showing who was really in charge. The Pope did not forget that humiliation.

Later, to divorce Josephine, Napoleon asked Pius VII to annul their marriage. Pope Pius VII was short and firm; he combined his refusal into one word: "Comediante!" Napoleon threw a temper tantrum and slapped the Pope in his face. For that punch, Pius VII yielded: "Tragediante!"

That was how "Comediante-Tragediante," a new form of literature and plays was born, comedy-tragedy in English. The story combines 2 great human emotions, comedy and tragedy, into one. To laugh or to cry, or do both at the same time, laughing through tears.

An Example of Comediante or Tragediante? Laugh or Cry?

It is not by accident that, to citizens' astonishment and sometimes amusement, the USA Congressmen and the Senators know only one thing—how to throw money at problems.

They keep throwing taxpayers' money at any problem, hoping and praying that the money, not the government, will "solve the problems." Because that is the only set of skills they have, knew it well, and use in their campaigns to get elected and re-elected.

Then, when they are elected to office, they apply their campaign skills—throwing money—at the wrong target in an attempt to solve national problems. In reality, solving national problems requires a completely different set of skills: creativity, innovation, and problem solving skills.

o   o   o

THE MORAL OF THE STORY

Comediante or Tragediente? To laugh or to cry? In literature and plays is an imitation of life and is taken from real life. Every day there are many moments or events around us when we laugh or cry, or do both, laughing through tears.

---

[1]   www.napoleon.org

11

SHORT STORY

How Did the USA Recover from the Great Depression of the 1930s?

o o o

How did the USA survive and recover from the Great Depression of the 1930s? There were 3 factors responsible for it: (1) World War II; (2) Noble President Franklin D. Roosevelt, FDR; and (3) The struggles, and tribulations of that generation.

(1) 1st factor: World War II, 1941–1945. Once the war started in 1941, unemployed Americans volunteered to go to war, and went to work in factories producing war machinery and supplies.

(2) 2nd factor: Noble President Frederic D. Roosevelt, FDR, 1933–1944. On March 4, 1933 the Americans elected the 1st and only the 4-term President, FDR, who came from a rich family and saw how ordinary Americans were suffering, not the rich capitalists.

People had no jobs (unemployment was 25% and in many cities much higher), no savings (the stock market crashed or inflation wiped it out), no money to buy food or pay utilities, no roof over their heads, depression, despair, no dreams, and no future.

Socialism was called to the rescue. FDR did not need to reinvent the wheel about socialism. Socialism was already invented and implemented in the Soviet Union, and the whole world knew the advantages of socialism over capitalism.

The basics of socialism were equal opportunity for all; women equal to men in education and wages; the right to work; 8-hour workdays; minimum and higher wages; free education and health care; safety net for seniors; no unemployment; pensions for all; and no homelessness, and many more. For example, after the November Revolution in 1917, the Soviet Union gave all women equal opportunity with men to vote, get a job, and receive an education.

The USA and Western world, afraid that their women would revolt after seeing Russia's women gain equal opportunity, they gave their women the right to vote: Austria, Poland, Czechoslovakia, and Sweden in 1918, Germany and Luxemburg in 1919, the USA in 1920, Britain in 1928, and Spain in 1931. France waited until 1944, and Italy, Belgium, and Yugoslavia until 1948.

FDR's major problem was how the nation could survive, not how rich capitalists could make millions from the national crisis and the war. FDR declared: "There will be no war millionaires."

In the 1930s, FDR did not reinvent the wheel; he took many features directly from the Soviet Union's socialist economy and implemented them directly into the USA's market economy. It was called the "New Deal."

It provided a social contract with the working class: Social Security, minimum wages, unemployment benefits, bank depositor insurance, federal home loan guarantees.

It also established new socialist agencies, including the Civilian Conservation Corporation, Public Work Administration, Work Progress Administration, and later Medicare in 1964.

Also, FDR proposed socialist decrees to Congress to establish in the USA socialist rights to a job, housing, education, and health care, but it did not pass the Congress.

(3) 3rd factor: Stoicism, endurance, sacrifices, and nationalism of the American's Greatest Generation who went through great suffering from high unemployment, soup lines, poverty, high inflation, loss of homes, and bankruptcies.

When World War II started, they marched stoically to serve in the war, and worked in factories producing goods, equipment, and supplies for the war.

After the war, they worked for low wages to build national wealth: consumer industries, new housing industries, transportation (bridges and roads), and a blossoming automobile industry. They sacrificed a lot for their country and for the future generations and took back very little for themselves.

o   o   o

THE MORAL OF THE STORY

To test the endurance and resilience of the American people, the stock market crashed in 1929, the USA economy collapsed, and the 1930s Great Depression started. The greatest human suffering in American history began. Unemploy-ment rose to 25% and higher resulting in soup lines, inflation, bankruptcies, despair, and no future.

Then fate intervened and sent 2 life preservers: (1) the Noble President Franklin D. Roosevelt was elected, and (2) World War II started. Fate remunerated the American suffering with a new and strong country, a prosperous new class—a middle class (the consumers) was born, and the USA became a world superpower. All beyond everyone's wildest imagination.

12

SHORT STORY

When Capitalism Ran Amok and Brought the Capitalist Economy to the Brink of Collapse, Socialism Was Called to the Rescue

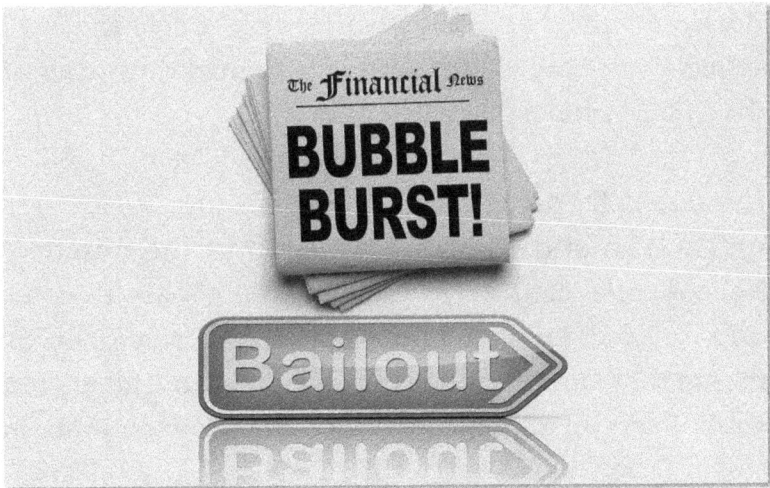

o o o

Unrestricted and unchecked American capitalism has run amok and 2 times brought the USA economy to the brink of collapse.

The 1st time capitalism ran amok was in the 1930s. It resulted in a national crisis called "The Great Depression of the 1930s," 1929–1939, that devastated the nation. Socialism was called to rescue the economy.

The 2nd time capitalism ran amok was in 2008, during what was known as the Financial Crisis. Capitalism (Wall Street, banks, and big corporations) robbed and impoverished the American middle class with 2 scams: "dot-com" and "subprime mortgages." Socialism was called in to rescue the economy from the ravages of the 2008 Financial Crisis.

The Great Depression of the 1930s in the USA and—Socialism Called to the Rescue

No one predicted or foresaw in the 1920s that an unparalleled level of human suffering would occur in America in the following decade. Unbridled, old capitalism ran amok, causing a severe economic crisis called "The Great Depression of 1930s," 1929–1939.

The economy collapsed, poverty was rampant, and unemployment rose to 25% (and in some cities was 80%–90%). This period was characterized by soup kitchens, bread lines, inflation, despair, depression, no dreams, and little hope for the future.

On October 24, 1929, the stock market crashed as stocks were bought on margin. To buy stocks, one was only required to put down 10% to get 90% on the margin. "Buy today, pay later" was the credit invention of the 1920s.

Scams were pervasive, such as fast money scams, stock market scams, and real estate scams (for example selling Florida swampland as lots to build homes). Scams were simple—a group of several rich capitalists met in secret. They pooled their money and bought a stock, for example, the RCA, (Radio Corporation of America). Naturally stock prices soared. Masses of small speculators hoping "to get rich quick from thin air" started clamoring to buy RCA stock at higher prices.

Once RCA's stock price reached $50–$60 per share, the rich capitalists would sell their RCA shares and the stock's price plummeted, wiping out many small speculators that bought stocks on margin. They got stomped out and were fried in the market.

Ironically, beginning in October 1929, the USA declared that, thanks to the stock market, the USA had become prosperous. The rest of the world followed by importing the USA market model hoping to replicate the USA's prosperity.

Then on October 24, 1929, the real market crash started. The market tumbled, a panic began, and everyone ran to sell stocks. RCA went from $100 per share to $20 per share and there were no buyers. Small investors— like workers, clerks, hairdressers, secretaries, and teachers, who dreamed of a comfortable retirement and paying their children's education—were wiped out.

The bottom fell out of the market. The game was over, providing a stark reminder of the reality of humility and human failure. What to do? How could the USA stop the economy from collapsing and alleviate the resulting human suffering? The answer was to call socialism to the rescue. President Franklin Delano Roosevelt, FDR, established a socialist New Deal.

Among the programs that made up the New Deal were Social Security, minimum wages, unemployment benefits, bank depositors' insurance (FDIC), and federal home loan guarantee. A number of socialist agencies were created as well, such as the CCC (Civilian Conservation Corps) to combat unemployment; the CWA (Civil Works Adminis-tration), to create jobs for the unemployed; and the SSA (Social Security Administration), which sought to combat widespread poverty among seniors.

The 1930s and World War II deeply changed Americans. A new America emerged, one whose view was characterized by dignity, honor, hard work, and pride.

The Financial Crisis of September 2008 Hit the USA and—Socialism Was Called to the Rescue

The 2nd greatest financial crisis in USA history occurred in September of 2008, once again bringing the USA economy to the brink of collapse. In the 1990s, President Bill Clinton removed many restrictions from the market and Wall Street went amok. "To get rich quick," Wall Street invented 2 scams, the "dot-com" and "subprime mortgages."

At that time, the middle class, by working hard all their lives, had accumulated over $3 trillion in their pensions, IRAs, and savings accounts. Wall Street was eyeballing those trillions and thinking about how to steal it. They invented a scam, called the "dot-com" where illusory company stocks were selling at inflated share prices.

These companies only existed on paper, generating little to no real earnings and often operating at a loss. In

2000, the "dot-com" bubble burst, causing the middle class to lose over $3 trillion in their pensions, IRAs, and savings—and 3.2 million Wall Street bankers and brokers became new millionaires.

Next, Wall Street invented their 2nd scam, 2000–2008, called "subprime mortgages." This time their target was unsophisticated population. From 2000–2008, Wall Street inflated the prices of new houses and condos for sale 3–5–10 times and then sold them to the unsophisticated population who had no money and no prospects of ever repaying such predatory mortgages. Soon they stopped paying these inflated mortgages.

Wall Street profited as they sliced and diced those subprime mortgages and sold them to investors in Europe and throughout the world. Iceland, Greece, Spain, and Italy nearly went bankrupt as a consequence.

The result was: the USA economy was on the verge of collapse and socialism was once more called to the rescue. The USA government, in an emergency and using the slogan "Too big to fail," bailed out Wall Street with $787 billion by passing the Emergency Economic Stabilization Act of 2008.

This bill put this debt on the shoulders of the American middle class to pay, and not on Wall Street crooks.

When under a capitalist system, the government or the Federal Reserve should not control the economy; it is private enterprises that do, and the free market will takes care of the economy. The USA government should not rescue one preferred industry, such as Wall Street, bankers, and big corporations at the expense of all others. Instead, preferred industries should rescue themselves. How?

Capitalists and Wall Street, who snookered $3 trillion from the American middle class and trillions more from their "subprime mortgages" scam, should give back all those trillions of dollars "earned" from their deceitful schemes big robberies and the USA government should prosecute these thieves.

Instead, the USA government took $787 billion from the middle class to bail out Wall Street. And as of today, not one of these Wall Street scammers, bankers, and big corporations is in the jail. Perhaps they are "too big to jail?"

But, the USA government puts 2.2 million Americans in prison for some petty crimes, such as shoplifting a candy bar from Wal-Mart because a person is poor or hungry, or for lighting up a marijuana cigarette.

Policymakers are fond of declaring, "We are a country of laws." Indeed, they are for small robberies that Main Street (the majority of the American population) commits. As for Wall Street's grand larceny laws do not apply, and the policymakers simply offer excuses and turn a blind eye.

The USA government has sold the country to Wall Street placing unsustainable debt on the shoulders of the American taxpayer. Today, the USA national debt stands at $19 trillion. It is not a matter of if the USA will go bankrupt, but when.

Today, the economies of the East are rising, while those of the West are drowning in debts and staying afloat through the use of even more debts. Today, China became the world's #1 largest economy, when measured by purchasing power parity.

o o o

THE MORAL OF THE STORY

When capitalism ran amok and brought the USA economy to the brink of collapse, socialism came to the rescue: a "New Deal" was established by President Franklin D.

Roosevelt in the 1930s. And a $787 billion bailout of Wall Street was authorized in September 2008 by President George W. Bush.

In the USA, capitalism, and its attendant social Darwinism ("survival of the fittest"), is only for the middle class and the poor population—"You are on your own, responsible for your life and actions, lose your job, go bankrupt, get sick, or become disabled—it is up to you whatever you live, or die."

At the same time in the USA, socialism is only for the rich capitalists—i.e. Wall Street, banks, and big business. Any time they bring the USA economy to the verge of collapse, the USA government calls on socialism to the rescue. The USA government bailed out the rich capitalists at the expense of the American middle class and poor. And not one of the rich capitalists was put in jail for their big schemes and thievery.

Why? Rich capitalists donate and finance all the USA government's official elections and re-elections and make the USA government policymakers millionaires.

SHORT STORY

13

What Is Capitalism, Socialism, and Communism?

○ ○ ○

What is capitalism? What is socialism? What is communism? I have had personal experiences with capitalism and socialism. I lived, worked, and was educated under both systems.

I was born and received my civil engineering degree in the Soviet Union. In 1967 I went to work in Africa, in Rwanda and Tanzania; there I worked with technical specialists and Peace Corps volunteers who came to Africa from all over the world to help the new African countries build their superstructures and economies after colonialism.

At the beginning of the 1970s, I came to the USA. When few women were engineers here, I was working as a structural engineer and had received 2 graduate degrees, a master's and a doctorate, in the USA.

Before 1991, the world was divided into 2 camps: capitalism and socialism. The leader of capitalism was the USA and under its umbrella were Western Europe, Japan, and Canada. The leader of socialism was the Soviet Union and under its umbrella were Eastern Europe, China, India, Africa, Asia, Cuba, and South America.

After 1991, the Soviet Union disintegrated and changed the whole world into one single system:

global capitalism. Today, the USA is still the leader of capitalism, with the whole world adopting capitalism too. Today all world is global capitalism.

What Is Capitalism?

What is capitalism? The foundation of capitalism is making money by all means possible—"Make money from thin air."[1] Capitalism is every man for himself, a form of social Darwinism: just get as much money as you can.

Property rights are above human rights under this system. There is no equality; there are classes, the rich and the poor. Resources, means of production, and profits are owned by private owners.

Capitalism is a system where a small number of wealthy people own and run the economy. Capitalism according to Karl Marx "is a dictatorship of the bourgeoisie." In a capitalist society "equal rights" are the everyday struggles of workers against bigotry, racism, sexism, poor working conditions, for health care, and for minimum wages.

Then after World War II, old American capitalism changed. It was replaced by a new American capitalism. Why? After World War II, a new class in the USA emerged, called the middle class, or the consumers, who were the majority.

It replaced old American capitalism with a new type of capitalism. This new American capitalism had 3 classes: rich, middle class, and poor. The minority rich, "have all"; the majority "the middle class"; and the poor, the "have not."

World War II was a blessing for the USA. After World War II, in 1945, the USA became a powerful country. How? After World War II, the Soviet Union was destroyed; for 3 years it had been fighting Hitler (1941–1944) on Russian soil and 26.6 million Russians were killed, almost all men between the ages of 18 to 50.

The Soviet Union defeated Hitler, liberated the country and Europe, and in June 1944 was marching on Berlin. The Red Army conquered Berlin on May 2, 1945.

The Soviet Union won World War II, but the country was ruined and leveled, and hunger and disease descended upon the vulnerable population. For the next 20 years, the Soviet Union was rebuilding their destroyed country with only women and old men. The situation was so dire that the Soviet Union did not participate in the Olympics until 1952. Europe was also ruined by World War II, and it took many years to rebuild it.

Meanwhile the USA, who did not participate in World War II for the first 3 years while the war was in the Soviet Union and Europe and not on American soil, had no competitors. German engineers and scientists, afraid of a Russian reprisal, all ran to the USA after the war. Also, European engineers, to escape the hunger and devastation in Europe, arrived in the USA. Here they developed the space program, innovations, new industries, and created the USA's national wealth.

The USA, unsure of itself and afraid of the greatest country in the world—the Soviet Union—after 1945 instigated a Cold War with the Soviet Union, by sabotaging its war recovery. America was also against the Soviet Union's system—socialism—which was for workers' rights and not for rich capitalists' profits.

What Is Socialism?

What is socialism? Americans are programmed and indoctrinated to believe that socialism is bad; they are afraid of socialism like a plague.

At the same time, they have socialism everywhere: unemployment benefits, minimum wages, Social Security, Medicare, food stamps, welfare, SSI disability, equal employment opportunity law, 8-hour workday, no child labor, and many more.

Additionally, many socialist federal agencies have been created to protect people: the EEOC (Equal Employment Opportunity Commission), OSHA (Occupational Safety and Health Administration), NLRB (National Labor Relations Board), FDA (Food and Drug Administration), FDIC (Federal Deposit Insurance Corporation), the ERA (Environment Protection Agency) and many more.

What is it about socialism that Americans are so scared of? Equality for all and the abolishment of private property. Everyone is equal in a socialist society; there is no rich or poor, no classes. The state is above the individual. A government runs the economy. The profits of any enterprise are equally shared by all people.

Socialism is a system where all resources and means of production are owned by the state and society; the state determines the distribution of resources based on people's needs in order to bring equality for all. People are compensated equally according to the amount of labor they do.

Karl Marx envisioned in socialism work and pay "From each according to their ability, to each according to their work." In a socialist society, at the beginning, there would still be remnants of capitalism and dictatorship of the people would be needed to transform society.

The foundation of socialism is equal opportunity for all people. After the Revolution of 1917, the Soviet Union issued decrees giving all women equal opportunity: the right to work; the same salary as men; the right to vote; and the right to enter universities. And by the 1960s, over 75% of Russian women graduated from universities versus 25% of Russian men; as for teachers, and physicians over 90% were women.

All people had rights for free housing, free education, free healthcare, free kindergartens, 8-hour of work per day, 15–30 days vacation per year, unlimited sick leave, women have 4-month maternity leave, universal pension, and retirement at age 50 for women and 55 for men. All enterprises were owned by the state, as were all parks, highways, railways, and harbors. The production and distribution of goods, as well as their price, were all decided by the state.

What Is Communism?

What is communism? Communism is an aspiration, a utopia that is never achievable, as it is based on idealism. According to Karl Marx's socialism theory, socialism is the 1st step, and communism is the 2nd step.

There are many examples where the socialist theory of Karl Marx was implemented: in Soviet Union, East Europe, China, India, Cuba, and in socialist countries in Africa, Asia, and in South America.

But, there is not one example in the world where a communist system was implemented. Why? In a communist system, there is no state. The state is not needed, and all means of production are owned by workers who belong to a community. Workers in a communist system have a high level of personal and intellectual development; they have noble traits of character.

They are in the last step—"self-actualization," as per Maslow's theory. Dignity, honor, and morality; great creativity, skills in problem solving; no prejudice; looking to help others and improve the quality of lives for all community members are all character traits of communists.

Abraham Maslow's theory of human development, the "Hierarchy of human needs and motivations" is applied here. His theory has 5 steps of human development: food, shelter, clothing; safety; social; self-esteem; and self-actualization.

When a person has achieved the 4 previous steps, he is on the 5th step, the most advanced—self-actualization. Communism requires high intellectual development for people which is not achievable for the majority.

The Western press misleadingly calls everyone who is not a capitalist, a communist, and all socialist countries are called communist countries. Adding to this confusion is the name of a political party. In socialist countries, they called their political party, the communist party.

When in the 19th and 20th centuries the revolts against inhumane capitalism occurred in many countries, when the revolutionaries organized into a party—they called it the communist party, they started the revolts.

Communism theory was taken from Karl Marx's revolutionary work and writing. It was one thing to theorize, and another thing to implement the theory in real life and see how, and if, it works.

The November 1917 Revolution in Russia implemented Karl Marx's theory of socialism. It overthrew the ruler of the tsar monarchy and established a socialist state of workers and peasants, the Soviet Union, or the USSR. Then, in 1949 China implemented Karl Marx's theory of socialism, then many more countries followed.

President Reagan's New Doctrine Was to Fight Communism and Resurrect Old American Capitalism

In 1981, to resurrect old American capitalism, President Ronald Reagan launched a new doctrine "To fight communism" and amplified the terminology "Communism." Why? To fight communism, which was against rich capitalists who were exploiting the poor "have not" people.

Also, Reagan lifted many government restrictions so the capitalist economy could run amok and regulate itself. He saw that "the government was a problem" for capitalism.

What is old American capitalism? For the first 200 years, until the end of World War II, 1945, capitalism in the USA was an old capitalism. It had only 2 classes: the minority rich, "have all"; and the majority poor, "have not"—the rest of the people.

Before the 1930s old American capitalism exploited poor farmers and factory workers, giving them low wages, long working hours, inhuman working conditions, child labor, and a short life expectancy of 45 years.

There was no middle class, and 30% of the population was poor farmers. Factory workers and farmers had no money to send their children to colleges on a mass scale. Capitalism kept the USA "separatist" from the rest of the world. The USA had no military strength to defend itself, and the size of its army was the same as the small country of Switzerland.

The Reagan propaganda machine, to resurrect America's old capitalism, launched a doctrine—"Communism." It repeated the word "Communism" again and again until the American population was indoctrinated into believing that indeed communism was the greatest threat to their existence.

President Reagan called the Soviet Union "Evil Empire." Why Empire? The Soviet Union was formerly the 700-year-old Russian Empire, which took 1/3 of Europe and 1/2 of Asia under its reign, and had 30 separate republics with different languages and cultures.

To shrink or eliminate the American middle class and make them pay for their middle class existence, the Reagan Administration lifted many restrictions from this new American capitalism.

Reagan fired air traffic controllers who went on strike; unions were broken and marginalized; "free trade" policies shipped manufacturing jobs overseas; taxes for the rich were cut; mental institutions were closed and mentally sick patients were thrown out on the streets, they become homeless and drug addicts.

Reimbursements to physicians were drastically cut: 90% of all physicians, who before Reagan were "solo practitioners," ran out of business and closed their offices; millions of patients were on the streets without physicians and HMOs (Health Maintenance Organizations) mushroomed; also physician associations grew exponentially.

Before Reagan, corporate CEOs earned less than 50 times the salary of the average worker. Under Reagan, this ratio went up to 100 times, and today it is 350 times.

o o o

THE MORAL OF THE STORY

Capitalism is uncertainty and unpredictability. Market economy is "expansion in all directions without restrictions," but it does not work.

Capitalism has: inflation, depression, financial crises, unemployment, and low wages. It has no free health care, no free college education, no free housing, no pensions for all. Capitalism is like a jungle—survival of the fittest—it is up to you to live or die.

Socialism is certainty and predictability; a centrally planning economy with 5-year plans, where you know what is going to be tomorrow or 1–5 years from now.

Socialism decrees gave an equal opportunity for all; women were equal to men in voting, in education, in work; 4-month maternity leave and free childcare for women, rights to have abortions; free health care; free education and cheap housing for all citizens; labor laws (8-hour workday), higher minimum wages;

prohibition of children labor; no dangerous working conditions; sick leaves; 2–4 weeks of paid vacation time; pensions and benefits for all, and many more.

Which system is better? Capitalism? Or Socialism? Capitalism is great when a person is lucky: born rich, received a private education, is healthy, young, and is well connected. Capitalism is a disaster when a person's luck runs out and the person becomes poor, cannot pay for his education, becomes sick, old, or experiences job loss. In this case, capitalism calls on socialism to the rescue to provide unemployment assistance, food stamps, welfare, medical assistance and Social Security and Medicare for seniors. That way, disadvantaged people are pacified and will not start a revolution to get rid of capitalism.

Is there a future for the entire world under the current single global capitalism system? What system is better? Capitalism? Or Socialism?

---

[1]   Examples: In the 17th century there was tulip mania in Amsterdam, where a tulip bulb was sold for as much as 5,000 guilders, then dropped to 100. In 2000 there was a "dot-com" scam where imaginary companies were created without any income and no possibility to ever have it; some of the stocks were sold up to $100 per share. When the market crashed, they dropped below $1 per share or went bankrupt.

SHORT STORY

14

3 Types of Economies:
Market, Planning, and Mixed

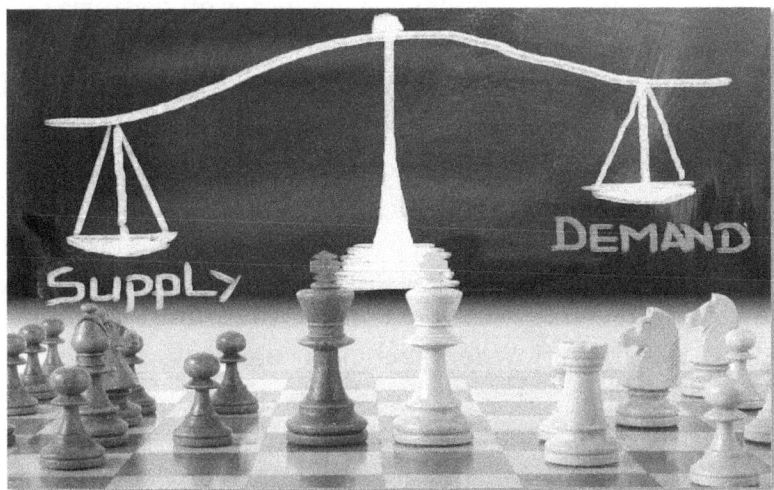

o o o

What is a free market economy? What is a planning economy? What is a mixed economy? Each of these 3 economies is associated with and designed for a particular type of political system.

There are 3 types of political systems: capitalism, socialism, and communism. (Communism is a utopian idea, or just an inspiration; it never existed in the past or present nor could it be in the future and is not discussed here.)

A free market economy was designed for a capitalist system. A planning economy was designed for a socialist system.

Today, a mixed economy is designed for all countries in the world: a mixture of a capitalist market economy and a socialist planning economy. Any time a free market economy is in crisis (inflation, recession, depression, unemployment, or economic crisis), a socialist planning economy is called to the rescue.

In this case, the USA government intervened to rescue a capitalist free economy with planning economy decrees: unemployment benefits, bailouts, handouts, food stamps, welfare, medical assistance, Social Security, and Medicare. Also, the Federal Reserve began managing the market economy by manipulating the interest rates in expectations that it would help the economy to recover.

A free market economy in its pure form in a capitalist system does not exist. Why? Because a free market economy does not work.

What Is a Capitalist Free Market Economy?

What is a free market economy in a capitalist system? A capitalist free market economy is "an expansion in all directions without any restrictions."

A free market economy is for the wealthy, healthy, and lucky individuals. But if you were born poor, did not get a good education, were laid off, got sick, or became disabled, you have no protection from becoming destitute. The rich get richer, and everyone else gets poorer.

A country with a free market economy has only one sector, the private sector. It is a free economy without any government interference. The government's role is limited to protecting the property rights of individuals and providing defense to the country.

The market will correct itself. Demand and supply rule the economy. The most successful market economy in the world, in size, has been the USA economy, and it is also the freest economy in the world.

In the USA, the private sector owns all of the country's resources. These owners are capitalists. Companies in the private sector compete with each other for a market share to receive the highest profit and get rich quick. For that, they take a risk and decide what to produce, for whom to produce, at what quantity, and at what price to sell. The major motivator for taking a risk is making a profit.

There is over 1 millions of lawyers to litigate the breaking of laws and settle any disagreements between competing companies. Workers work harder for rich capitalists because they are afraid of losing their jobs. To run the market economy, the USA government has many laws and regulations on the books and the Congress continuously creates new laws and regulations with the motto "We are a country of laws."

To implement the laws and regulations, the government has a formidable system in place: police, lawyers, courts, judges, and prisons.

Disadvantages of a Market Economy
There is no equality in the standard of living and there is economic uncertainty. The society is divided into 2 extreme classes: capitalists, "have all," the minority; and workers, "have not," the majority. Again, the rich get richer and the majority of the population gets poorer.

To squeeze out more profits, capitalists exploit workers by paying them low or minimum wages; have longer working hours; have unhealthy working conditions, and provide no health care, no education, no insurance, and no housing. Workers are employed as long as the high profits keep rolling in. As soon as the high profits stop, there are mass layoffs of workers and as a result, increased unemployment.

Who pays the unemployment benefits? The USA government. Not the capitalists. For example, in 2014, the Hewlett Packard Corporation's profits decreased and they immediately laid off 50,000 workers to keep their profits up.

Capitalists also produce harmful products and services as long as they generate a profit for them. They do not produce the much needed products and services for the population if they do not receive much of a profit from them. Moreover, their production wastes a lot of resources and they don't care. As long as it brings in a profit, they will continue manufacturing them. The government must enforce the rights of their citizens with police, courts, and judges.

Furthermore, capitalists are big political donors and their money elects and re-elects politicians; they spend millions and billions of dollars lobbying politicians and making politicians millionaires.

Corruption also makes capitalists richer. In short, capitalists buy politicians to run their billion and trillion dollar scams and fraud schemes and in turn, they receive no punishment. For example, President Obama has not put any of those capitalist-crooks in jail.

When unrestricted capitalism runs amok through scamming the population and looting the government, the result is—economic crisis: inflation, recession, depression, and crisis.

And who suffers the most? It is the American people who are burdened with unsustainable national and personal debts.

And what do the capitalists do next? They go to the USA policymakers asking them to rescue them and policymakers immediately bail their donors out. Why and how? The capitalist system and its free market economy are designed in theory to run without any USA government interference. Free market forces will take care of any economic crisis, that is, "expansion in all directions without restrictions." It is socialism and a socialist planning economy that is run by the government.

There is a double standard and irony here: a capitalist free market economy was left running amok until it ran the USA economy into the ground.

Then, the USA government called on the socialist economy for help. The USA government (as a socialist government) intervened into the capitalist free market economy and bailed out the capitalists with over $700 billion dollars, as was the case in September of 2008. But this is socialism! In capitalism, the USA government should never interfere in the market economy. And this vicious circle of economic crises keeps repeating itself again and again.

What Is a Socialist Planning Economy?
What is a central planning economy in a socialist system? It is a planning economy designed for only one sector, the public sector.

The government socialist planning economy was created by the Soviet Union after the Russian Revolution of November 1917. A socialist planning economy is the production of goods and services according to the needs of the population, not by its wants.

The government's central planning committee determines the needs of the population and then issues 5-year and 10-year production plans. The government owns all the means of production and properties while the people own only a small piece of land and the house sitting on it. The government decides what to produce, and which factories will produce it. The government decides the prices for goods and services and they are the same across the country.

A planning central economy has no inequality in income among its citizens because it is designed for everyone. Goods and services are distributed according to personal needs, not by their wants, therefore there is equality for all. Everyone has the same rights to a lifetime job, to have a free education, free healthcare, and free housing.

If someone gets sick or becomes disabled, no problem, he will receive pension benefits, regardless of how long he or she worked, or what his or her salary was. No one is destitute, or sleeps under a bridge. The government takes care of its citizens from birth to death.

All socialist countries took the Soviet Union's central planning economy as a model for their planning economies. And so did the USA, Western Europe and today the whole world; they implemented many decrees from the Soviet planning economy into their economies.

Today, all economies in the world, including the USA, have 2 sectors: the private sector and the public sector.

The Soviet Union was the leader of a socialist central planning economy until 1991, when it disintegrated. Today only Cuba and North Korea still have the Soviet planning economy.

Advantages of the Central Planning Economy

The Soviet Union implemented decrees of Equal Employment Opportunities in 1918; as a result, Russian women received the same salary as the men and universities accepted students not by their sex, but by the highest scores in the entrance exams. That is why in the Soviet Union, 75% of the women graduated with university degrees versus 25% of the men. As for teachers and physicians, over 90% were women.

Moreover, there was no unemployment. The central planning committee knew how many jobs were needed and how many people to train for particular jobs. For example, the Soviet Union needed only 2,000 lawyers per year, so the universities produced only this number. Of course, the number of students competing for the 2,000 places was high.

There were also labor laws and subsidized services. This included an 8-hour workday, working only 40 hours per week, paid vacations 15–30 days per year, paid maternity leave for 4 months, and health spas paid by the government for 14–30 days.

Beauty salons for manicures, pedicures, and facials, they were of a high quality and were located on every corner of the street, were cheap (subsidized by the government), and the majority of the women used them at least once a week.

Public transportation was cheap and also of a very high quality. There was almost no crime—6 murders per year, no rapes, and no burglaries. There were also no guns in the country. Even the police had no guns and not many police cars.

Furthermore, there was no inflation, recession, or depression. The currency, the Russian ruble, was a closed currency. It could not be converted into another currency and could only be used inside the country for trading. With a closed currency, there was no worry that inflation from another country would come inside. No recession or depression.

A planning economy could not run amok because there was optimal production and no uncertainty. The quantity of goods and services were produced according to the needs of the population.

Healthcare, housing, and a secondary and university education were free to all citizens. Only utilities required payment, but they were very cheap, at less than 1% of one's monthly salary and even less for retirees.

Housing was allocated by needs, not by wants. For example, a single person could receive only a 1-bedroom apartment free, as per his needs, but, if he wanted a bigger one, then he could buy himself a condo and pay for it. The government built condos and did not make a profit on them, which is why all condos were cheap and affordable.

Also, pensions were given for all citizens, and the retirement age for women was at age 50 and men at age 55. Life, cars, and house insurance did not exist. In short, the government took care of its population from birth to death.

Disadvantages of the Central Planning Economy

The government owned everything: oil, raw resources, land, factories, malls, supermarkets, and transportation, parks, and many more. Only one sector existed, which was the public sector. No one could own private property, but any citizen could have a home and a summerhouse, a car or a sailboat. All this could be bought or sold. Moreover, the standard of living did not increase as fast as in a market economy. One could not be a millionaire.

But there was an elite at the top: government officials, engineers, scientists and sportsmen. An engineering salary was 2–3 times more than a physician's salary. The best students went into engineering.

The same trend is occurring today in the world: engineering is the most prestigious profession in the world, except in the USA.

What Is a Mixed Economy?

What is a mixed economy? It is an economic system where a happy combination of the 2 sectors exists:

a private sector (from capitalism) and a public sector (from socialism). After the Soviet Union (a socialist system with a central planning economy) disintegrated in 1991, it changed the world—into one single system, global capitalism.

In reality, a pure free market economy in a capitalist system does not exist, because it does not work. Instead, it is a mixed economy.

Today all countries in the world, including the USA (a capitalist system with a free market economy) have only one type of economy—a mixed economy. In a mixed economy, a happy combination of the 2 systems, capitalism and socialism, exists side by side.

The 1st system, which is the capitalist free market economy, includes the private sector, has free enterprise, private ownership, and the ability to produce profits.

The 2nd system, which is the socialist planning economy, has a government public sector to control unemployment, inflation, recession, depression, and economic crises when capitalist free market enterprise runs amok.

The government provides a social safety net for its disadvantaged population with unemployment, minimum wages, Social Security, Medicare, medical assistance, welfare, SSI, and food stamps.

Why do the USA and all other countries in the world today not have a free market economy? Simply put, a free market economy does not work.

The USA as early as 1918 took a decree from socialism after the Russian November 1917 Revolution, and granted the same decree to American women. Therefore for the 1st time in American history, women were allowed to vote in 1920.

Then in the 1930s, the USA, during the market economic crisis—the 1930s Great Depression—implemented many socialist decrees from the Soviet Union's planning economy. The Soviet decrees were in President Franklin D. Roosevelt's "New Deal" programs.

These "New Deal" decrees gave a safety net to a destitute American population: social security, minimum wages, unemployment benefits, bank depositor insurance, and federal home loan guarantees. New agencies were also created: the Civilian Conservation Corporation, the Public Work Administration, and the Works Progress Administration. President Roosevelt also proposed certain decrees to Congress—the socialist's right to jobs, housing, and health care—but these did not pass. Later in 1964, Medicare was created.

In August 2008, when the USA market economy ran amok and went into economic crisis, the USA government, in order to save the economy, intervened and rescued Wall Street with socialist planning economic decrees.

They gave over $700 billion in bailouts to capitalists such as big corporations and bankers who were "too big to fail" and put those debts on the shoulders of the American taxpayer. When in a capitalist free economy, the USA government should not have interfered; they should have let the free market economy take care of itself and fail.

The Federal Reserve also intervened and started running the USA economy in pegging interest rates at 0% so that the banks and corporations could get rich and re-invest these profits back into the economy to "create jobs."

That did not materialize however. Instead, banks are now sitting on over $3 trillion they took from savers and retirees, and are hoarding this money. They had no intention of re-investing it into the economy. Why?

Remember, they robbed the nation and paid themselves billions in salaries and bonuses. If they had re-invested this $3 trillion back into the economy, they would have had no more money to pay themselves inflated salaries of $10–$50 million each. And then what? To ask the USA government again to bail them out? They are clever foxes because they knew how to rob the people of their money for their own personal enrichment.

Western Europe, after the oil embargo in 1973–74, switched to a mixed economy. They had no alternative. By the 1960s, they had lost all their colonies.

Western Europe had no oil or raw resources. The oil embargo quadrupled oil prices and their economy went into a depression. To survive, they switched to a mixed economy, which was a happy combination of the 2 systems: the private sector and the public sector.

o o o

THE MORAL OF THE STORY

What is a free market economy? It is "an expansion in all directions without restrictions."

A capitalist free market economy, if left unchecked, will run amok and bring economic crisis. In the USA examples, the

Great Depression 1930s and the September 2008 Financial Crisis, the USA government called on the socialist planning economy for help to save the economy—it bailed out big companies and banks. Why? A capitalist free market economy does not work.

What is a planning economy? Such an economy has only one sector, a government sector, which has a central planning committee that decides what to produce, how to produce it, for whom to produce it, and the price to sell it.

Planning economy was in the former socialist countries: the Soviet Union, Eastern Europe, China, India, Cuba, and socialist countries in Africa, Asia, and South America.

After 1991, when their leader, the Soviet Union disintegrated, all socialist countries wanted to become rich and millionaires. To achieve this objective they switched from a planning economy (public sector), to a mixed economy—all to get rich and at the same time have government protection from destitution.

That is why today, almost all countries in the world have a mixed economy. A happy combination of 2 systems: a capitalist market economy (private companies and individuals are running the economy) and a socialist planning economy (a government managing the economy).

The main difference between the mixed economies of different countries in the world is in the amount of government intervention. For example, in the USA, the share of government intervention is 38%, while in France it is 53%.

SHORT STORY

15

There Are 3 Types of American Capitalism: Old, New, and Global. What is Old Capitalism? New Capitalism? Global Capitalism?

o   o   o

There are 3 types of American capitalism: (1) Old capitalism which occurred from the 17th century–1940s; (2) New capitalism, from 1940s–1991; and (3) Global capitalism from 1991– present.

What Is "Old" American Capitalism?

"Old" American capitalism lasted from the 17th century to the 1940s. For the first 200 years, until the end of World War II in 1945, capitalism in the USA was "old."

It had only 2 classes:

1) The "have all" rich capitalists, the minority; and

2) The "have not" majority, the rest of the population.

Before the 1940s, American capitalism exploited poor farmers and factory workers by giving them low wages, long working hours, and inhumane working conditions, employed child labor, and the resultant effects of all of this was an average life span of 45 years.

There was no middle class; 30% of the population were poor farmers. Factory workers and farmers had no money to afford university schooling for their children on a mass scale. Capitalism kept the USA "separatist" from the rest of the world; the USA had no strength to defend itself, and the size of the American Army was the size as the army of a small country, such as Switzerland.

What Is a "New" American Capitalism?

After World War II "old" American capitalism changed. It was replaced by a "new" American capitalism from 1940s –1991. But why?

After World War II, American veterans received free education and discounted mortgages. New housing was built on a mass scale, and factories were working at full capacity to produce goods and war equipment for the USA and for export to war devastated Western Europe.

German and European engineers and scientists arrived to the USA from war-devastated Europe and developed technologies to compete with the Soviet Union during the Cold War. Dwight D. Eisenhower brought innovations from Europe: bridges, roads, and highways; the USA started building thousand of bridges and millions of miles of highways. The automobile industry blossomed; and new suburbs were born where millions of single family homes were built on a mass scale.

After World War II and during the Cold War, a huge new class of Americans was created—the middle class or consumers—the majority of the population. The middle class became secure, educated and prosperous. It acquired stability, and were selfless as the Marshal Plan, which was massive aid to rebuild Europe, evidenced.

As for "old" American capitalism? After World War II, American capitalism changed dramatically with the entrance of the new class, the American middle class.

Now American capitalism had 3 classes:

1) "Have all" rich capitalists, the minority;

2) The "middle class" consumers, the majority;

3) The "have not" the poor population on public assistance, the rest of the population. Plus, for older Americans to live in dignity, Social Security (1934) and Medicare (1964) were established.

As for impoverished Americans, the "have not," free medical assistance, welfare, and food stamps were established.

What Is "Global" Capitalism, 1991-Present?

From 1991, America's "new" capitalism disappeared forever. It was replaced by "global" capitalism. After the Soviet Union disintegrated in 1991, it changed the whole world into one single system—"global" capitalism.

The arrival, of "global" capitalism pushed the USA and Europe economy spiraling down. Today 1 in 2 Americans are living in poverty, or near poverty line.

Western Europe countries in decline; they have no oil, and no raw resources. The same time they have huge unemployment 25% and higher, huge debts, no jobs, and no future. Why?

Before the Soviet Union disintegrated, the world was simple. It had 2 systems: capitalism and socialism. The leader of capitalism was the USA, it had under its umbrella Western Europe, Japan, and Canada, approximately 700 million population in total. They were only the buyers of oil and raw resources on the world market.

Before 1991, the socialist countries were living below their means; they did not trade with the USA and Western Europe, nor did they buy oil or raw resources on the world market. After the Soviet Union disintegrated in 1991, the whole world adopted global capitalism and everyone wants to "get rich quick."

Today the world changed severely. The USA, Western Europe, Japan, and Canada in ferocious competitions competing with 7.2 billion people for oil and raw resources on the world market (versus 700 million before).

The result: in the last 20 years they have depleted world oil and raw resources; polluted the planet, and converted it into an impending ecological holocaust. American capitalists moved tens of thousands of their factories to other continents to get even richer from cheaper labor and low cost of raw resources.

Numbers of millionaires and billionaires is growing, but the world population getting poorer every day.

o o o

THE MORAL OF THE STORY

There are 3 types of American Capitalism: old, new, and global. Nothing in life is constant, except a change. Change happens every day. There are many world events that triggered changes.

Even capitalism keeps changing its form in accordance with prevailing times and circumstances. Until the 1940s the form of capitalism that existed in the USA was old capitalism with 2 classes, the "have all" rich minority class; and the "have not" poor class, the rest of the population.

After World War II, a new class was born, a middle class, or consumers, and to accommodate this new middle class, a form of capitalism changed into new capitalism.

Then, after the Soviet Union disintegrated in 1991, it changed the whole world from 2 systems (capitalism and socialism) into one single universal system—capitalism. And capitalism changed its form into—global capitalism.

SHORT STORY

#16

"Look Through the Window." Or, Marie Antoinette and President George W. Bush

○ ○ ○

King Louis XVI of France Was Fighting the British on American Soil by Financing the American Revolution

The British were French old enemy. In 1776, the American Revolution began against the British in North America, on American soil. The French King Louis XVI had a strategy that it was much better to fight French old enemy, the British, on American soil than on French. He was fighting the British on American soil by financing the American Revolution.

In 1778, France recognized America as a sovereign nation. In modern currency, the French spent a total of approximately $13 billion on the American Revolution. To pay for it, the King levied unsustainable war debts on the French people, and imposed heavy taxes on them until the taxes decimated them. Poverty, disease, hunger, and despair tumbled down on the nation.

Soon, the French people became impoverished; they could not take it anymore. There was no way out, except one, to get rid of their despotic monarchs, King Louis and Queen Marie Antoinette. They started their own revolution, the French Revolution. The mob stormed the Bastille prison, freed all the political prisoners, and the French Revolution began in 1789.

The French Revolution transformed France's monarchy into a new Republic, whose one slogan, among many other was: 'Liberté, Égalité, Fraternité' (Liberty, Equality, Fraternity) for all people. Later, these revolutionaries authorities executed the King and sent Marie Antoinette to the guillotine.

Marie Antoinette, the Queen of France, Never "Looked Through the Window" to See How Her People Lived

The French Revolution caught Marie Antoinette, 1755–1793, the Queen of France, by total surprise. She had no clue what was going on outside of her palace. Royal intrigues, luxury, and pleasure absorbed her personal life.

When the French Revolution started and angry crowds stormed the palace, wild rumors spread that Marie Antoinette was out of touch with the reality around her to such an extent that she asked her court: "Why are the people revolting?" Her court replied: "They are hungry, they have no bread." "Give them cake," the Queen suggested.

If only she "looked through her window" she could see that her husband, King Louis XVI, wrought back breaking debt and taxes upon his people, all to help the American Revolution when fighting the British. War debts impoverished and decimated the French people and they revolted and overthrew the French monarchy.

President George W. Bush, as the French King Louis, Started Afghanistan War to Fight Terrorists on Their Soil

More than 200 years passed after the French Revolution, 1789, and history repeated itself on another continent, North America, in the USA, under President George W. Bush in 2000-2008. As the French King Louis XVI, President Bush, started Afghanistan war to fight terrorists on their soil.

On September 11, 2001, al-Qaeda attacked the World Trade Center and the Pentagon, an attack on USA soil. Almost 3,000 died in the attack and 836 responders including firefighters and police.

The mastermind was the Afghanistan Taliban and the commander was Osama bin Laden, who was a rich Saudi Arabian elite, conducting a holy war against the USA and the Western culture he despised. Bin Laden built his reputation on the combat experience against the Soviet troops in Afghanistan in the 1980s. At that time the USA and Western Europe supported Bin Laden's fight against the Soviet Union war in Afghanistan from 1979–1989.

Immediately after 9/11, President Bush called the attack "acts of war" and demanded the Taliban deliver

Bin Laden and destroy all al-Qaeda (bases in Arabic). Afghan Muslim clerks answered the USA's demand to stop the "harassment of innocent people" and if the USA invaded Afghanistan "jihad becomes an order for all Muslims."

The USA did invade Afghanistan on October 7, 2001 marching into the war under the banner "Operation Enduring Freedom," and was fought there until the end of 2014.

In 2003, President George W. Bush started another war in Iraq, 2003–2011, for the false reason that Saddam Hussein had WMD (Weapons of Mass Destruction). Over 4,500 Americans were killed in Iraq. The USA did not win these 2 wars and pulled out from Iraq in 2011 and from Afghanistan in 2014.

Insurgencies in Afghanistan increased as the USA was pulling out. In Iraq, today a civil war is in full force and the USA started bombing Iraq again along with Syria in August 2014.

The cost of these 2 wars? By the end of 2013, over 7,000 American troops died in Afghanistan and Iraq, the majority of whom were young men whose lives were still ahead of them. Approximately 633,000 were wounded, and 2.3 million Americans have fought in these 2 wars.

Unaccounted for are American troops who returned home and killed themselves as the result of their combat duty, or troops who committed suicide on non-active duty. The Department of Veteran Affairs does not report suicide rates among veterans. Also unaccounted for are the over 3,000 military contractors who died in the 2 wars.

Over 23,000 uniformed Afghans, Iraqis, and other USA allies have died since 2001. Wars destroyed Afghanistan and Iraq, started civil wars there, increased the numbers of insurgencies, and killed many thousands of civilians.

The financial cost was over $4 trillion in terms of USA military expenses from 2001–2014. Not counted are medical costs and soaring veterans benefits in the Department of Veteran Affairs and military expenses in the Department of Homeland Security.

On May 2, 2011, Osama bin Laden was killed by the CIA and by Navy Seals in Pakistan. The irony was, before 9/11, the Soviet Union had been fighting Bin Laden in Afghanistan, but the USA, with its Western European allies and Saudi Arabia were supporting Bin Laden to fight the Russians.

Osama bin Laden built his reputation on his combat experience against the Russian troops in Afghanistan in the 1980s. He always carried a Kalashnikov rifle, claiming he took it from a Russian solider he had killed.

Then, when the Soviet Union disintegrated in 1991, Bin Laden moved to Afghanistan, made the al-Qaeda an international Islamic enterprise for terrorism, and started a holy war against his biggest supporter—the USA and the Western culture he despised.

President Bush, Like Marie Antoinette, Never "Looked Through the Window" and Was Surprised by the USA Financial Crisis in September 2008

Like Marie Antoinette, President George W. Bush never "Looked through the window" and was surprised by the USA Financial Crisis in September 2008.

During George W. Bush's Presidency, 2000-2008, tax receipts fell and spending increased. In 2008, over 75% of Americans believed that the USA economy was in bad shape and was "headed in the wrong direction."

Not President Bush. When in February 2008, President Bush addressed the nation, he declared: "Our economy is strong." Even today, from time to time, some TV stations still show this particular segment of President Bush's reassurance that "Our economy is strong."

In September 2008, the USA's economy collapsed and unemployment, debt, housing foreclosures, poverty, and unaffordable gas prices descended on the American people.

The economic collapse caught President Bush's administration by total surprise. Also surprised were the USA government, the lawmakers, the Federal Reserve, economists, business consultants, advisors, and "the best intellectual minds." That was, no one predicted it, or saw it was coming. The Chairman of the Federal Reserve Mr. Greenspan was in shock: "Who could have predicted it?"

They all, like Marie Antoinette, more than 200 years before, had been absorbed in their personal grandiosity, on how to grow their personal fortunes and the fortunes of American banks and corporations and never looked "through their windows" to see what was going on around them, in the USA economy, in the nation, and how the American people lived.

If they only had looked outside, they could have seen that the USA economy did not collapse overnight. The fact was that it started collapsing years before, in 2000–2008, all due to the following 10 major, widening cracks.

It was not a matter of if they would become wide enough to collapse the USA economy, but when. The cracks were the following:

1. The USA population and employment growth between 2000–2008. The population grew in 8 years by 23.6 million from 281.4 million in

2000, to 305 million in 2008; this is an average growth of 3 million per year or by 8.3%.

2. Unemployment. What did the population growth mean for unemployment? It meant that, just to keep unemployment at the same level as in 2000, the economy had to create 23.6 million new jobs in 8 years.

At the same time, only 7.2 million new jobs were created during this 8-year period versus 23.6 million new jobs needed.

Approximately 3 million people were entering the labor force each year for the first time. Annually, only 0.9 million new jobs were created on average per year, short of 2.2 million new jobs needed per year. There was a total shortage of 16.4 million new jobs during this period.

3. Americans on food stamps. During his presidency, President Bush added 10 million Americans to food stamp rolls, from 17 million in 2000 to 27 million in 2008. Unemployed Americans went to collect food stamps.

4. Consumer debts, housing underwater, foreclosures, and bankruptcy in September 2008. Consumers' personal debts in September 2008 were at a historic peak of $12.7 trillion.

Home values plunged by 50%; over 7.6 million American homes were underwater, and 2.1 million Americans filed for bankruptcy.

5. Military expenditure. President Bush started 2 wars, Afghanistan in 2001 and Iraq in 2003; the total military expenses in 8 years were $3.85 trillion.

   The objective was to fight terrorists on their soil, not on American soil. Exactly the same as the French King Louise XVI's strategy was, who paid for the American Revolution by heavily taxing French people to fight his enemy, the British, on American soil, and not on French.

6. The USA national debts doubled. It grew from $5.0 trillion at the beginning of Bush's Presidency to $10.0 trillion in 2008, or a $5 trillion increase in 8 years, or by 100%.

7. Tax rates are extremely low—30% versus 70% in the 1970s and 90% in 1950s. As the result of low taxes—unsustainable national debts are growing quickly.

8. The USA real GDP in trillions of dollars. It grew from $12.7 in 2000, to $14.6 in 2008; increased by $1.9, or by 15%. When at the same time, the national debt grew by $5.0 or 100%.

9. Wall Street scams. At the same time, Wall Street was booming and became rich overnight. It manufactured the new "dot-com" scam, 1996–2000, in which they robbed over $3 trillion dollars from the USA middle-class pensions, IRAs and savings while 3.6 million Wall Street crooks became new millionaires overnight.

10. Wall Street's 2nd scam. From 2000–2008, Wall Street invented a 2nd scam "subprime mortgages."

The target was the unsophisticated population who had no savings and could not afford to pay 3–5–10 times inflated predatory mortgages. Soon they stopped paying and went bankrupt. Wall Street then sliced and diced those "subprime mortgages" and sold them to many European countries, who are all now in dire economic straits: Iceland, Greece, Spain, Portugal, Italy, and many others. While 2.8 million Wall Street crooks became new millionaires from "subprime mortgages" fraud.

The fact is: for the USA economy to grow and expand, it needs real innovations. Innovations that create and build national wealth: superstructures, infrastructures, new products, services, and new industries.

Innovations in turn create new jobs. With the income from new jobs, people spend, buying consumer goods and housing, and pay taxes. Taxes in turn pay national debts.

Wall Street "dot-com" and "subprime mortgages" scams produced no national wealth. Wall Street crooks just robbed the middle-class of their hard-earned pensions, IRAs, and savings and also robbed European countries and put money into their own pockets. Then, not to pay any taxes on this money, they hid it in Swiss banks accounts, the Bahamas and Cayman islands, and invented many more tax loopholes.

Surprise came in September 2008 when the USA economy collapsed. Mr. Henry Paulson, President Bush's Secretary of the Treasury and the ex-Goldman Sachs CEO (whose personal wealth is over $170 million made on Wall Street) paid an emergency visit to the Congress and the Senate, asking them to bailout Wall Street to rescue the USA economy.

Lawmakers, in a hurry, bailed out the bankers and corporations to the tune of $787 billion. "Too big to fail" was a pretext the USA lawmakers used to justify their quick actions and rescue of Wall Street crooks, bankers, and corporations who destroyed the USA economy and American middle class. Then under President Obama's administration, not one of those crooks has been sent to jail for their criminal acts. "Too big to jail?"

President George W. Bush and all his "best economic brains," economists, consultants, the Congress, the Senate, and the Federal Reserve, like Marie Antoinette before them, never "looked out their windows" to see what the outside world, in this case, how the USA economy and American people were doing.

If they had looked outside, they would have easily seen the above 10 major economic fissure that were becoming disastrous cracks, which had developed gradually in 8 years, from 2000–2008.

O O O

THE MORAL OF THE STORY

"Look through the window" and see what is going on in the outside world. Otherwise, face the consequences like President Bush's administration did. In his administration no one was "looking through the window" to see what the USA economy was doing.

The result was that the USA economy collapsed in September 2008. When the fact was that the USA economy did not collapse by accident, nor did it collapse overnight. It took years for 10 cracks to develop and widen and for the structure of the economy to collapsed.

One does not need to be a rocket scientist to see it, just by "looking through the window" and finding out what is going outside, how the USA economy is doing and its impact on average American lives.

If President Bush's administration, lawmakers, the Federal Reserve, and economists "looked out their windows," they would have seen the cracks in the above 10 major economic factors. The cracks were widening, and not if, but when they would became wide enough to push the USA into Financial Crisis. That happened in September of 2008.

17

SHORT STORY

President Barack Obama's
2 New Doctrines

○ ○ ○

"I do not give to people hell, I just tell the truth and they think it's hell."

Harry S. Truman, 33rd President of the USA

Today, President Barack Obama is pursuing his 2 new doctrines:

A). "World disorder" and

B). "National disorder."

The "World disorder" doctrine seeks to keep foreign countries in political, social, and economic turmoil. Recent examples of the USA's wars and turmoil are: Afghanistan, Iraq, Libya, Syria, and since from February 2014, Ukraine.

The political stability and peace of those foreign countries were destroyed and replaced by everyday turmoil, destruction, killings, and millions of refugees. On a daily bases, President Obama is personally, in charge of his "World disorder" doctrine.

The "National disorder" doctrine aims to keep the USA bankrupt and sinking, like the Titanic, into trillions of dollars of more unsustainable debt and push millions of more Americans into poverty. President Obama put Wall Street, banks, big corporations, and the Federal Reserve in charge of his "National disorder" doctrine.

A) "World Disorder" Doctrine

Why was the doctrine of "World disorder" created? To allow big donors who are financing political campaigns—the big American corporations, banks, military industry, and private contractors—to get richer. How is the doctrine financed? By the USA's $800 billion in annual military expenses.

Who is paying for $800 billion of military expenses? The already impoverished American people are paying for those military expenses, and for the wars and political turmoil that the USA government started in faraway foreign countries.

Today, the burgeoning national debt is $19 trillions, or over $50,000 for every American man, woman, and child. Many Americans were killed, wounded, and traumatized from the recent wars and chaos in Afghanistan, Iraq, Libya, and Syria.

Who is in charge of the "World disorder" doctrine? President Obama is; he also serves as a self-appointed world policeman. The tragic fact is: the USA had no money to finance any world disorders. How long is the USA going to print paper money to finance President Obama's "World disorder" doctrine?

After the terrorist attack on September 11, 2001, the USA started fighting several wars in Afghanistan, Iraq, Libya, and Syria: no one war was won. Just the opposite happened.

Today, all those countries are in turmoil; civil wars, death and distraction, millions of refugees, and radical Muslims are winnings.

The cost of these wars? The USA is bankrupt with over $19 trillion in national debts; this debt is a ticking time bomb. There is no more wealth, no more real money, and the USA just continues printing paper money to finance foreign wars and distraction.

How President Obama Remunerated the World Who Gave Him the Nobel Peace Prize

How did President Obama pay back the world for giving him the Noble Peace Prize and the $1 million attached to it? He made the world a more dangerous place and is drumming up militarism with his doctrine of "World disorder" to keep foreign countries in political, social, and economic turmoil.

Today he even has an objective, as many previous invaders, the last of whom was Hitler, to destroy Russia and the Russian people. To implement his objective, in February 2014, he shamelessly and arrogantly staged a coup d'état in Ukraine to stir the war with Russia.

A) Coup d'état in Ukraine in February 2014 Was a Pretext to Destroy Russia

In 2014, the war in Afghanistan was winding down, and President Obama started looking around the globe to find another foreign country, a victim, to implement his new doctrine of "World disorder" to start military turmoil, so the joint venture between the USA government and his political donors of big corporations, banks, and military industry keeps going.

In 2014, President Obama's victim became Ukraine. In Kiev, the capital of Ukraine, on the "maidan" (a city square), a demonstration against government corruption started peacefully. Then, the USA interfered, and launched the coup d'état against the legitimate Ukrainian government, spending billions of dollars on it. Paying $1,000 per month in cash to fascists, Nazi, thugs, and criminals, and $3,000 per month to their gang leaders, when the average salary in Ukraine is $300 per month.

President Obama put in charge his State Department representative, Ms. Victoria Nuland to conduct coup d'état in Ukraine. She arrived in Kiev's maidan, distributing cookies and encouraging fascists, Nazi, and criminals to topple the legitimate Ukrainian government with violence, destruction of government buildings, and the killing of innocent civilians by putting themselves in charge. They did.

Ms. Nuland's telephone conversation, as the Ukrainian coup d'état commander, went viral. The USA bankrolled a mercenary army in place consisting of Nazi and Jihadist to fight in Ukraine against "pro-Russians."

They are not pro-Russians, they are Russians; 17% of the population in Ukraine is Russian. In Crimea, 60% of the population is Russian and that area was a Russian territory until 1954 when Nikita Khrushchev, a President of the Soviet Union, gave Crimea to Ukraine.

Even Senator McCain arrived in Kiev to support the violence. He addressed violent criminals on the maidan, stating that the future of Ukraine is with Europe, not with Russia.

The fact is: Ukraine never was with Europe. Ukraine, roughly the size of France and a population of 42 million had been under the rule of imperial Tsars of Russia for over 200 years. Then, after the November 1917 Russian Revolution, it became an independent republic under the Soviet Empire, and was one of the Soviet Union's 30 different republics.

Let's imagine if President Vladimir Putin of Russia orchestrated a coup d'état in Washington. And sent his State Department representatives to Washington to appear next to the White House giving cookies to violent mobs who have burned the American government buildings, killed police and peaceful demonstrators, toppled the government, and put fascists and radicals in charge. And some top Russian officials would arrive to Washington to keep the violence up and make statements to mobs and thugs that the USA must be with Mexico and not with NATO. This is an analogy to what Ms. Nuland and Senator McCain did in Ukraine.

President Obama's coup d'état installed an illegitimate government in Ukraine; they are fascists, Nazi, right-wingers, aggressive, violent and the backward minority from West Ukraine, or 17%–20% of the Ukrainian population.

During World War II, they fought on the German side against Russians. That is how with President Obama's help and money, using drugs and drinking vodka, they became violent beasts killing innocent people, unarmed police, burning government buildings, and destroying everything in their path.

Just look at news footage and see their terrifying actions, how beasts dressed in human clothes went on a rampage every day on the maidan and later in Odessa. Chasing demonstrators into buildings, they threw Molotov cocktails inside and cooked demonstrators inside alive. Those who wanted to exit were finished with bats on the ground.

That is how and why such a small, violent minority of fascists, Nazi and criminals were able to overthrow the legitimate Ukrainian government.

Immediately, to humiliate and bring the Russians in Ukraine to their knees, this violent West Ukraine fascists minority announced: "From now on, Ukraine is one people, one language, and one religion."

Interpretation, 50% of the population who speaks only the Russian language must learn the Ukrainian language overnight. And 80%–85% of Ukrainians who are Christians and practice Russian Orthodox also must convert to Catholicism overnight.

Even more, those fascists asked Chechens (who in 2004 killed 400 Russian school children inside their school) and Jihadists for help—to join them to fight "pro-Russians" in East Ukraine.

The Russian population in the Eastern and Southern parts of Ukraine did not accept such humiliation from the Western Ukraine fascist minority and revolted seeking their own independence, just like what occurred in Kiev months before.

And whom did President Obama blame for his ill-orchestrated coup d'état? The President of Russia, Vladimir Putin. President Obama flew to Europe many times to organize, instigate, and persuade his European puppets and NATO allies to rally against Russian President Putin.

Hunter Biden, a son of USA Vice President Joe Biden, was hired as a director by a Ukrainian energy company by promoting energy independence from Moscow. He is a director whose business is pending before the White House, in this case before his father, Joe Biden. Where are the laws, conflicts of interest, ethics, dignity, and honor?

B) "National Disorder" Doctrine

President Obama's "National disorder" doctrine seeks to keep the USA bankrupt and sinking, like the Titanic, into trillions of more dollars of unsustainable debt and push millions of more Americans into poverty. He is not in charge of this doctrine. Instead he allowed Wall Street, banks, big corporations, and the Federal Reserve to manage the USA economy on a day-to-day basis and to implement his doctrine.

President Obama's Unfulfilled Campaign Slogans and Promises

When President George W. Bush was in charge of the country, disillusioned with his presidency, the American people wanted a drastic change.

Here, Presidential Candidate Barack Obama appeared and filled in the people's wants and dreams. He ran his 2008 campaign on powerful slogans and many promises such as: "Change we can believe in," "Yes, we can," "Hope," "Betting on America," "Winning the future."

When he was a Senator, he voted against the war in Iraq. One of President Obama's 2008 campaign promises was that his administration would be the most transparent in USA history.

During President Obama's 2012 re-election campaign, a previous slogan "Change we can believe in" was replaced with "Forward we can believe in." He promised to stop the Afghanistan war, improve the lives of Main Street (middle class), punish Wall Street, and free prisoners at Guantanamo Bay.

Did Nobel Peace Prize Winner President Barack Obama fulfill his campaign slogans and promises? No, not one, none. Once in office, he threw out his campaign slogans and promises and replaced it with his 2 new doctrines: "World disorder" and "National disorder."

How President Obama Remunerated the American People Who Made History by Voting for Him

In 2008, Presidential Candidate Barack Obama won and made history. He became the 1st African-American President in the USA thanks to inspired American people who gave him a chance, voted for him, and believed that he would live up to his campaign promises and voters' expectations.

They hoped he would be honest and change the country. This historic event reverberated throughout the world, and the world awarded him a Nobel Peace Prize. They did so, believing that due to such a historic event as his election, he will do something good for the world in return.

And how did President Obama remunerate the American people who voted for him and the world who made him a Nobel Peace Prize Winner accompanied by a monetary prize of $1 million?

President Obama's payback to American people: he expanded NSA spying—from a small number under President Bush—to cover the entire USA population, all 316 million of them, plus the world. All so his big donors will continue getting rich every year from the $800 billion the government gave to them, and they would continue donating to political campaigns. He added 20 million Americans to food stamp rolls (versus 10 million under President Bush). Today 47 million Americans are on food stamps. President Obama added $9 trillion dollars to national debts in just 5.5 years (versus $5 trillion by President Bush in 8 years).

He increased military expenses by 136% per year versus Bush. Today, total national debt stands at $19 trillion while he continues to put $1.1 trillion per year more debts on the already impoverished American people.

More Scams Are Added to Destroy American Middle Class: Saving Accounts with 0% Interest Scam

Saving accounts with 0% interest are impoverishing seniors. This Federal Reserve scam, invented by the Chairman of the Federal Reserve, Mr. Ben Bernanke, has been going on for years, robbing savers and seniors and giving that money to crooked bankers and Wall Street. Interest on savings accounts has been kept at 0%. With no earnings from interest accounts, seniors started living from their principals, exhausted it, and now are living below poverty.

Banks made over $3 trillion from this scam, and according to the press, are "hoarding and do not want to invest" the money on creating new jobs. The reason bankers are hording this cash is to pay for their multimillions-dollar salaries and bonuses. This time, they are afraid the USA government is not going to bail them out as it did in September 2008 to the tune of over $700 billion.

Inflation Scam
The USA government is "cooking books" when calculating inflation. The USA has almost no inflation, according to the cooked books. In reality, inflation is 10%–20%. Just go to a grocer, and see that food prices are rising all the time, and not by just 5%–10%, but by 30% –100%.

Housing Scams
Every decade, housing prices in the USA zigzag sharply up and down. Single homes from a lower range of average price at the $40,000–$70,000 to a high of $250,000–$800,000, when the salaries of population in the last 20 years stopped growing.

Prisons Scams

Today the USA prison population is staggering—it stands at 2.2 million. It cost the taxpayers annually $45,000–$50,000 per prisoner. And who gets rich from this high numbers of prisoners? Big private contractors who are managing the prison population. They get billions every year.

In 1980, the prison population was below 0.5 million; today it is 2.2 million, or nearly 5 times increase. Corrupt courts and judges, bribed by private prisons, are putting armies of innocent people into jails so private prisons can make even more money from the USA government. The USA has 4.5% of the world's population, but 25% of the world's prisoners.

Doctors Are Scamming Medicare and Financing Top Democrats

One of President Obama's 2008 campaign promises was that his administration would be the most transparent administration in USA history. Just the opposite happened. The White House kept top-secret Medicare payments to doctors, who were big political donors.

Only after a subpoena from a newspaper in April 2014 did the White House release information regarding Medicare payments to doctors in 2012. Articles in *Bloomberg*[1] and *USA Today*[2] published on April 9, 2014 both shockingly revealed how American doctors are blatantly robbing Medicare.

In 2012, Medicare paid over $77.0 billion to doctors. Medicare paid over $1.0 million apiece to 4,000 doctors and medical professionals in just 2012.

And the White House kept the pay by Medicare to physicians sealed, a top secret, so the public could not learn that, for example, Medicare paid tens of millions each to 3 doctors, all of whom are top Democrats donors.

The New York Times on April 9, 2014 reported:[3] Dr. Salomon E. Melgen, ophthalmologist in Florida, has only 900 patients but received $21 million from Medicare in 2012, has a private jet. "Dr. Melgen's firm donated more than $700,000 to a Majority PAC, a super PAC run by former aides to the Senate majority Leader, Harry Reid, Democrat of Nevada."

Dr. Asad Qamar, an interventional cardiologist in Florida, was paid over $18 million in 2012 and donated over $250,000 to President Obama's campaign. Dr. Michael C. McGinnis, a pathologist from New Jersey, received $12.6 million in 2012 from Medicare. His donations to top Democrats are top secret.

President Obama Put nor One Wall Street Crook Into Jail

"We are a country of laws," Washington policymakers like to announce and state to the camera. Indeed they are.

Except this law does not apply to the Wall Street rich, the policymakers' big donors. They committed massive frauds and crimes, such as robbing over $3 trillion from Main Street pensions, IRAs, and savings accounts in Wall Street's "dot-com" and then from "sub-prime mortgages" scams. From those 2 scams alone, over 6.4 Wall Street crooks became new millionaires.

And when they collapsed the USA economy, President Bush and President Obama bailed them out in 2008 to the tune of $787 billion, with an explanation that those institutions and companies were "Too big to fail."

And...under President Obama not one Wall Street crook went to jail for their big heists, proving to be "Too big to jail." Why? Wall Street financed President Obama's campaigns. To raise money, many times he had dinners in the mansions of Wall Street hedge funds managers.

Instead, he put millions of Americans into jail for petty crimes, so private prisons could plunder the USA government and become even richer.

Number of Accidental Deaths in the USA

It is a sad irony—the USA government spent trillions of dollars "looking for terrorists" and "fighting them on their soil," so they would not harm Americans, or repeat the terrorist attack of September 11, 2001 that killed over 3,000 Americans.

The result: except for Osama bin Laden, not many terrorists were found. At the same time, President Obama spent trillions of dollars "to save American lives" from potential terrorists.

How sincerely does President Obama care about American lives? If President Obama cared just a little bit, he could do something to cut down the accidental death number of 500,000–600,000 Americans killed every year inside of the USA, which is far more than the number who perish at the hands of terrorists.

Statistics: Every year, 500,000–600,000 Americans die from accidental deaths. Over 500,000 from medical mistakes: 150,000 from physician mistakes (number of suits filed against physicians), 210,000–400,000 patients died from hospital mistakes,[3] and 100,000 from drug side effects. And over 120,000 from other accidental deaths: 15,000 homicides, 38,000 from drug overdoses, 35,000 in car accidents, and 38,000 committed suicide.

Or, in the last 13 years, beginning from September 11, 2001, over 6.5 million Americans died from accidental death (13 years x 0.5 million =6.5 million.) How many terrorist attacks could kill this number of Americans? Or what number of terrorists' nuclear bombs?

Analogy: In August 1945, the USA dropped 2 atomic bombs on Hiroshima and Nagasaki in Japan, killing 129,000 Japanese.

Instead, President Obama sought to "fight terrorism" and "change the regime" to divert the attention of American people from the monumental and grave economic and social problems inside the USA.

o   o   o

THE MORAL OF THE STORY

Even though the USA has an unsustainable ticking national debt of $19 trillion—President Obama continues implementing his 2 new doctrines of "World disorder" and "National disorder," all to keep foreign countries in political, economic, and social turmoil.

An army of Washington lobbyists are lobbying the White House, the Senate, and the Congress to start new military turmoil, wars, and coups d'état. So the big corporations, banks, and military industry would continue getting richer from the USA government. In peacetime, he has increased the military budget by 136%. President Barack Obama's 2 doctrines are destroying the country and American people.

President Obama's "World disorder," as all previous examples of "regime change" show, ended up replacing top dictators with even worse one. Regime changes have produced no solutions and merely served to generate infightings for power between different factions, causing the countries to dissolve into civil war and anarchy. The everyday civilian population is killed, suffering, and thousands or millions have become refugees in neighboring countries.

When the world is in disorder, the USA enterprise of big companies, military industry, and private contractors get rich quick—by robbing and looting the USA government, evoking people suffering and putting the burden of unsustainable debt on the USA and on the shoulders of the American people. In return, those big donors are financing political campaigns.

Today, President Obama's major objective is to destroy Russia and the Russian people and he is using a coup d'état in Ukraine as a pretext for doing so.

Russians are stoic and proud people; they prefer to die with dignity rather than to live in humiliation and under repression. That is why in the 700-years history of the Russian Empire and the Soviet Union no other empire or country ever conquered Russia, despite many trying. Numerous invaders marched on Moscow but could not subjugate it. The Russians defeated all of them and never failed. One rule of the warfare books—never march on Moscow—applies equally to President Obama.

"Money talks" is how the saying goes. To get elected and re-elected, corrupt politicians need big corporations and military industry donors to finance their expensive campaigns. In return for political donations, the USA government (the White House, the Senate, and the Congress) remunerates their big donors with $800 billion in annual military expenditure.

President Obama's other doctrine of "National disorder" has produced a disaster. Millions of

Americans who are eligible to work have no jobs; 45 million have no health insurance; 100 million received 1–8 or more different types of government assistance; 47 million are on food stamps; 1.1 million homeless; and 2.2 million in prisons; and billions are spent every year on fighting an impending ecological holocaust.

Every year, over 500,000 Americans are dying from accidental death; the quality of healthcare lags far behind all other industrial nations yet is the most expensive.

Americans have over $17 trillion in personal debt, and $1.1 trillion in student loans. Today the USA is the greatest debtor nation in the world, it has over $19 trillion in ticking national debts and 1 in 2 Americans live in poverty or below poverty line.

The Federal Reserve, for many years, has kept interest rates at zero, so bankers could get rich, while seniors, who live on a fixed income, are now unable to retire and are poor. Banks are hoarding trillions of dollars so they can pay themselves billions of dollars in salaries and bonuses and do not need to ask the USA government to bail them out again.

And the USA government did not care or notice the above tragic suffering of the American people. Why? They are selfish and care only about themselves; they have only one objective: to become rich quickly from occupying government positions. Just see how the politicians went in a short time from rags (before their elections) to riches (after they were elected).

The Noble American President Franklin D. Roosevelt during the Great Depression of the 1930s and World War II strictly implemented his law that "There will be no war millionaires." Because every war benefits only the rich while the rest of the people are suffering.

Do you know that there are many thousands of decent, honest and patriotic Americans who are willing to give their lives to become congressmen, senators, and president, so they could serve their country with dignity and honor, and put the country first before their selfish monetary greed.

Unfortunately, they have no chance, as they lack the millions of dollars needed to finance their political campaigns, and no big corrupt enterprises would donate millions to support dissent, nationalistic, and honorable Americans.

The USA's fate is the same as many before it, when the great empires and great superpowers for centuries ruled the world then suddenly disintegrated and disappeared. Recent examples: British empire disintegrated in 1947 and the 700-year-old Russian Empire and the later Soviet Union disintegrated in 1991.

Today, the USA is a sinking Titanic—it is not a question of if, but when it will sink? How long is the USA going to print paper money to finance President Obama's doctrine of the "World disorder?"

How long will "National disorder" scams and schemes continue impoverishing American people so the rich keep getting richer and the poor keep getting poorer?

---

[1]   "Top Medicare Doctor paid $21 Million in 2012 Data Show," by Caroline Chen and Sophia Pearson, April 9, 2014, Bloomberg News.

[2]   "7 doctors got more than $10 million from Medicare in 2012," by Peter Eisler, Meghan Hoyer and Alex Beall, USA Today, April 10, 2014.

[3]   "Political Ties of Top Billers for Medicare," by Frances Robles and Eric Lipton, April 9, 2014, The New York Times. How many patients die from medical mistakes in the USA hospitals? Between 210,000–440,000 patients each year, as per the Journal of Patient Safety. In any given year hospital care contributed to the death of 180,000 patients on Medicare alone, as per The Office of the Inspector General for the Department of Health and Human Services. Medical mistakes are the 3rd leading cause of death in the USA (#1 heart disease, #2 cancer.)

SHORT STORY

18

Why Is the NSA Spying on All 316 Million Americans and the World?

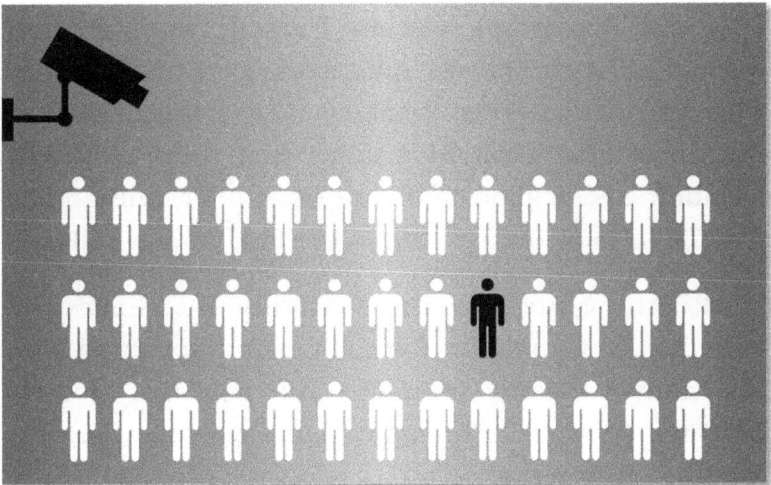

O O O

"Any society that would give up a little liberty to gain a little security will deserve neither and lose both."

Benjamin Franklin

In the USA 2008 was a historic event. Americans elected their 1st African-American President, Barak Obama. This event attracted the world's attention, elevating him to become a Noble Peace Prize Winner with a $1 million award.

Americans and the world optimistically believed that President Obama would live up to their hopes and aspirations and do a lot of good for his citizens and the world. That never happened.

Why did Americans elected Barack Obama? They wanted a drastic change. Americans were disillusioned with President George W. Bush for starting 2 wars in Iraq and Afghanistan, resulting in high unemployment, for adding $5 trillion to the national debt, and adding 10 million more Americans to the food stamp rolls.

To fill in the wants, needs, and aspirations of Americans, Presidential Candidate Barack Obama appeared with his many idealistic promises and powerful slogans. Slogans, such as: "Change we can believe in," "Hope," "Betting on America."

One of his campaign promises was that his administration would be the most transparent in American history. Believing him, American voters made history and elected him.

How did President Obama remunerate American voters? How did he keep his promise to be "The most transparent administration in the USA history?"

Here's how: with the NSA (National Security Agency), he ambushed Americans on 2 fronts, personal and financial. He ordered mass spying on the personal, everyday lives of all 316 million Americans and at the same time he made Americans pay for the programs that were spying on them! Every year, President Obama earmarks billions of dollars to the NSA to spy on Americans.

The NSA is a top-secret organization that originated during World War II. After the September 11, 2001 terrorist attack on the World Trade Center in New York City and on the Pentagon in Washington, D.C., new IT systems were created to deal with the flood of information from new technologies like the internet and cell phones.

Whistleblower Edward Snowden revealed the existence of these data mining programs. After the terrorist attack, there was a need to have the NSA conduct surveillance to prevent future attacks.

Common sense dictates targeting just that minuscule number of the USA population that is under suspicion of terrorist activities. The NSA spying grew, and President Obama expanded it to the entire USA population, all 316 million of them, as well as to the rest of the world.

One does not need to be a rocket scientist, just have common sense, to conclude that there is no reason for this and it makes no sense to spy on all citizens.

Why do they need to spy and listen to ordinary meaningless everyday telephone conversations? For example, Cindy: "Hello, what are you doing?" Carole: "Oh, nothing, just watching TV. What about you?" Cindy: "Oh, standing in line, in a supermarket." Where is the terrorist plot, breaches of national security, or hidden codes?

But the NSA is listening constantly and stores billions of such types of innocuous conversations. Why? Not by an accident, there was a reason for that. What was the reason behind mass spying on the all innocent population? A simple one—financial enrichment.

The answer lies in the number of people under surveillance. You see, at the beginning, the NSA was spying on a very small number of people, probably only 10–20 thousand suspicious ones—and dollar payments to the big USA corporations for their spying services was very small. Then, to get rich quick, they designed the NSA new scam—"Spying on the entire population of 316 million Americans." Later, they expanded this scam to the world. The NSA began spying on many foreign countries and millions of their citizens.

That is how and why the USA's big corporations began putting $10.8 billion every year (that we know of) into their pockets in 2013. The corporations are robbing and looting the USA government, who in turn added this amount to the $19 trillion of growing unsustainable national debt.

Question: How many people did the NSA need in order to gather, process, and analyze all the telephone conversations and emails of 316 million citizens? Many thousands, plus armies of networks and computers and millions of feet of cable. That is why the NSA did not find many real or imaginary terrorists in recent years. Why?

There are few if any American terrorists, probably a few, or several at most. And even if there are more, it is impossible to find a real terrorist; it's as difficult as trying to find a needle in a stack of hay. The NSA paid big corporations $10.8 billion in just one year, 2013, and did not find any terrorists!

How many billions in total did the NSA pay to corporations for years of spying on its citizens? It is a closely guarded secret President Obama has kept from the American people who are paying for this NSA financial scam to spy on them. So much for President Obama's empty campaign promise that his administration "would be the most transparent in American history."

o o o

THE MORAL OF THE STORY

The NSA is spying on the entire American population, all 316 million of them! Why? Comediante or Tragediante? To laugh, or to cry?

How many terrorists has the NSA caught from such massive spying? None that we know of. Why is it spying on such a massive scale? For one and only one reason, to get rich from the USA government.

To win the Presidency, during his campaign, Barack Obama transformed himself into an inspiring idealistic candidate. He spoke using created uplifting slogans and sounds bites, and made many promises to the American people telling them exactly what they wanted to hear. Once in office, he changed back to his real personality, character, and beliefs. He started remunerating the big donors for his campaigns—big companies and the military industry—with financial scams at the expense of the USA, and, in 6 years of his presidency, put an additional $9 trillion of unsustainable national debt on the shoulders of the American people.

And how did President Obama remunerate the American people who voted for him, and the world who made him a Nobel Peace Prize Winner accompanied by a money prize of $1 million?

President Obama's pay back to American people is: he expanded the NSA spying from a small number under President George W. Bush to spying on the entire USA population, all 316 million of them.

This was done so his big donors, the big American companies and military industry would continue getting rich from the $800 billion he gives them every year from the USA government. For that, he has increased the USA military spending by 136% compared to President Bush. And when he leaves the office, they will remunerate him with millions of dollars so he can join the multi millionaire club of recent Presidents.

More payback. In his 6 years in office, President Obama added 20 million Americans to the food stamps list and added $9 trillion to the national debt. President Bush, during his 8 years in office, added 10 million Americans to the food stamps list and added $5 trillion to national debt. Today, there is no light at the end of the tunnel.

In short: Why is the NSA spying on all 316 million Americans and the world? Simple. The NSA is a secret joint venture between President Obama's administration and their big donors, big USA corporations, banks, and the military industry. They get richer, and American people get poorer.

19

SHORT STORY

Big Scams in the USA That Are Destroying the American Middle Class, Seniors, and the Nation

o o o

It was September 23, 2008, a hot midday in California. To escape the heat, I went inside my home and turned on the news.

When I saw what was on the news, I froze with disbelief. The USA Congress was giving $700 billion of the national wealth and taxpayers' money to bail out Wall Street.

I glanced at the clock; it was past noon in California, or 3:00 p.m. in Washington D.C. I was in a hurry, on fire, and on a mission. Nothing could stop me. I turned on my computer and started firing off letters, and before 5:00 p.m. Washington time, I faxed it to over 20 prominent USA Senators and Congressmen. One typical example can be found below.

Scams #1 and Scam #2.
Or, 2 Wall Street Scams: "Dot-com" and "Subprime Mortgages"
September 23, 2008

The USA Senator and Democratic Presidential Candidate Barack Obama

United States Senate

713 Hart Senate Office Bldg. Washington, DC 20510

Via fax at (202) 228-4260

RE: PLEASE STOP PRESIDENT BUSH'S $700 BILLION BAILOUT of WALL STREET

And to whom has the Congress given the responsibility to manage the $700 billion Wall Street bailout? The fact is that to the FOX to guard the chicken coup: to Henry Paulson—Wall Street architect from Goldman Sachs! Please fire him.

Dear USA Senator and Democratic Presidential Candidate Barack Obama:

The fact is, the best years are behind the USA; it is now a sinking Titanic. Why? It has not happened by accident. Please look out the window to see what has happened in the last 10–15 years. Please see the following facts, below.

(1) Before 1995, the USA went through many technological revolutions with innovations and inventions that transformed the country, brought value to the society, and improved the quality of living: the industrial revolution, arms and space races, infrastructure boom, innovations in consumer goods, and many more.

This technological revolution, of over 200 years, created many millionaires and by 1995 there were 3.6 million millionaires in the USA.

(2) After 1995, besides the World Wide Web, there were no new technological revolutions, or new inventions,

nor new innovations that added value to the country. But, at the same time, from 1996–2008, 6.4 million new millionaires were created!

(Today, the total number is 10 million millionaires.) No inventions, no innovations, the USA is a sinking Titanic and at the same time, 6.4 million new millionaires were created in the last 10 years. How has such phenomenon occurred? Where did those millionaires come from? It has come from 2 types of Wall Street innovation-scams, the "dot-com" scam and the real estate "subprime mortgages" scam.

The 1st Wall Street innovation-scam was called "dot-com" (in 1995–2000). The target was trillions of dollars "Main Street" had accumulated in pensions, IRAs, and savings accounts. For that, Wall Street created imaginary paper companies ("dot-com"), cooked the books (i.e., inflated profits) of existing companies, and then sold them to Main Street for up to $400/share. Soon, however, those prices crashed to a penny/share.

The fact is, Wall Street produces nothing, contributes nothing, nor does it add any value to the society/ country. Instead, it lives from society, by using skills and manipulations to "advise" Main Street as to what they should do with their hard-earned money.

The fact was, by 1995, Main Street, by working hard all their lives, had accumulated trillions of dollars in their pensions, IRAs, and investment accounts. Wall Street was itching to rob Main Street of their trillions and launch their own innovation-scams, as above. The result was, by 2000, Main Street lost trillions of dollars in pensions and IRAs.

At the same time, Wall Street created 3.6 million new millionaires from their "dot-com" scam. (In 2001, the total number of millionaires in the USA was 7.2 million.)

After 2001, Wall Street faced a new problem, the "dot-com" scam became obsolete. Main Street had no money left, and from then on Main Street did not trust Wall Street. So, Wall Street invented a 2nd scam, as described below.

Wall Street innovation-scams called: "subprime mortgages," 2001–2008.

Wall Street created imaginary money by slicing/dicing selling subprime mortgages to an unsophisticated population.

Their objective was to sell 3–5–10 times inflated mortgages to an unsophisticated population, a population that could not afford it and had no money to pay. They sold 3–5–10 times inflated mortgages for crumbling old houses that had no structural life left in them. The facts were that all engineering structures are designed for a certain lifespan.

That meant that wood frame single-family houses were designed for "0" (zero) years. Such houses would last until the first tornadoes, hurricane, mudslide, wind, snow, earthquake, fire, flood, or any other natural disaster occurred.

At the same time, reinforced concrete apartment buildings were designed for 25 years; reinforced concrete commercial buildings for 37 years; reinforced concrete bridges for 40–45 years. After these life spans, they could fail at any time.

Majority of cars are designed for 10 years. After that period, the car value is a few hundred dollars; a personal computer is designed for 3–5 years, appliances for 5 years.

The result was millions of the unsophisticated population could not afford to pay for 3–5–10 times inflated mortgages. Foreclosure, bankruptcy, and the housing market collapse were the realities.

The winners during this time were the 2.8 million new millionaires Wall Street created from 2001–2008 through the "subprime mortgage" scam. (In 2008, the total number of millionaires in the USA was over 10 million.)

Summary: Wall Street is a meth lab: it produces nothing, nor does it add any value to the country or to society. It is a meth lab that constantly designs scams-innovations to rob unsophisticated populations, destroying the economy, sinking the USA, and lobbying the Congress and the Senate to approve their scams.

Question: What was going on? Why weren't those robbers in prisons as Enron's founders and other scam artists were? Why did you not ask them to return the trillions of dollars they had in their personal accounts from their scams?

For the Main Street (middle-class population)—"We are a country of laws." Any type of robbery, regardless of how small it is (for example, $5–$10 shoplifting from Wal-Mart), is a crime and is punished by years in prison.

As for the Wall Street crooks who became multi-millionaires by robbing trillions of dollars from Main Street and destroyed the USA economy for many generations to come, you just salute them by giving them another $700 billion from the Main Street! What about taking back the trillions they robbed from the population? And send all Wall Street crooks to prison for a mandatory 10–20 years minimum sentence for grand larceny?

Thank you. I appreciate your attention.

Sincerely,
Alla Gakuba

o o o

How Wall Street Resurrected Donald Trump from Bankruptcy. Or, How a " Dead Cat Bounced"

After 3.6 million Wall Street crooks became overnight millionaires from their "dot-com" scam, they went shopping for real estate in their own city and headquarters, New York City.

It also happened to be the domicile and real estate headquarters of Mr. Donald Trump.

With easy money, Wall Street crooks vacuumed up and bought all of Mr. Trump's real estate in New York City—and suddenly reversed Mr. Trump's fortunes from bankrupt to billionaire, propelling him from rags to riches.

Now, after such luck, Donald Trump's lost self-esteem was resurrected and his old personality sprung back to life. Soon, he started parading around on TV again, on various shows, as he did before many years ago.

He started speaking with such reassurance as if he, and not the Wall Street crooks, had changed his life from bankruptcy and billions of debts into the brand new status of a billionaire and prosperous real estate tycoon.

Scam #3.
The Federal Reserve scam "0% Interest Rates"

After Wall Street's "dot-com" scam crashed the stock market or "the bubble burst," the USA capitalist economy spiraled downward. The USA government did not leave the capitalist free market economy to correct itself. (The foundation of the capitalist market economy is "expansion in all directions without restrictions.")

Instead, it called the socialist economy to the rescue! For that, the Federal Reserve interfered and started rescuing the failing economy. How?

Mr. Greenspan, the Chairman of the Federal Reserve, immediately changed 100-year-old economic law. He instituted "0% interest rates" for the American people. Now they, the middle class, must rescue the economy at their expense and carry the burden on their shoulders.

Not the Wall Street crooks who robbed over $3 trillion dollars from the American middle class' pensions, IRAs, and savings, and 3.6 million Wall Street crooks become overnight millionaires from their "dot-com" scam.

From now on, Mr. Greenspan made sure that middle class people would earn "0% interest rates" on their money market and savings accounts. In this case, banks, having free access to people's money, would start loaning back to people (their own money) at 4%–25% interest for mortgages, cars loans, personal loans, and credit cards.

Soon, according to Mr. Greenspan's "0% interest rate" law, banks would have a windfall; they would accumulate trillions of dollars in the banks' coffers. And banks, having that money, would reinvest back into the American economy, creating new jobs, and producing new products and services, allowing the USA economy to recover. *That was just Mr. Greenspan's wishful thinking theory.*

Unfortunately, his theory never materialized! Why? Now banks and Wall Street started itching, wondering how to steal that earned interest money, trillions of dollars, from the banks' coffers and to put into their own pockets.

For that they invented the #2 scam, called it "subprime mortgages." Remember that by that time, the middle class had no more money. All their life savings were lost to Wall Street scam #1, "dot-com" and 3.6 Wall Street crooks became new millionaires.

So, now banks and Wall Street targeted an unsophisticated population, who had no money and no possibility to have any in the future. Crooks sold them "subprime mortgages" to buy overpriced single homes and condos at inflated prices, 3–5–10 times. Soon, they could not afford to pay the inflated subprime mortgages, stopped paying, filed for bankruptcies, or simply walked away. The Wall Street crooks and bankers faced the reality that their "subprime mortgages" scam did not work, as it did not bring them a lot of real money.

(Let's remember that crooks are dealing with the real money. They cannot print money, only the Federal Reserve can.) Next, the Wall Street crooks re-engineered their "subprime mortgages" into another type of scam. How?

They sliced and diced these mortgages and sold them in blocks across the world. Soon, Iceland, Greece, Spain, Italy, and others went bankrupt, and 2.8 million Wall Street crooks and bankers became new millionaires!

Parallel to this scam, another scam was created and implemented—multimillion dollar salaries to bank presidents and administrations. From now on, and as of today, the banks' coffers simply became their presidents' and administrations' personal coffers. Without any shame, they simply looted it as soon as the money started pouring in.

Before the "subprime mortgage" scam, the banking profession was a very dull and low paid profession. Not many bright people went to work for banks. I remember that my banker friends in the 1980s were looking up to me. I was in an exciting profession, and my engineering salary was much higher than their banker salaries were.

Before, a banker's annual salary was $20,000-$40,000, with no bonuses. Not in the 2000s, for example, when the president of Bank of America started receiving a $50 million annual salary and over $50 million annual bonuses, over $100 million in total. Thousands of dollars salary simply became millions.

When Mr. Greenspan introduced "0% interest rates" to rescue the USA economy, it seems that he had a flick of dignity and honor. He thought about the seniors, the retirees, the savers, and what a devastating effect the "0% interest rate" will do to them. He knew that it simply pushes the majority of seniors, who live on fixed income, into poverty and into food stamps.

To soften the devastating effect of his "0% interest rate" on savers and seniors, Mr. Greenspan made a special provision for them in his law. Instead of depositing all their saved money into savings and money market accounts in banks where they earned 0% interest, they had another option or alternative.

Seniors and savers could invest their saved money into the USA government I-bonds, $60,000 maximum each year per account and pay no tax on earned interest until withdrawals. I-bonds were created to counterbalance the inflation.

The total interest on I-bonds consists of 2 parts. The 1st part is a fixed rate interest that is established by the Federal Reserve 2 times per year, in May and in November, at say 3%. The 2nd part is a variable rate, depending on the rate of inflation, that is established in May and in November, at say 5%.

Then, for example, the total I-bond interest rate for May is 8% =(3% fixed rate +5% variable inflation rate). This 8% interest rate continues forward. Besides seniors, these I-bond interest rates and $60,000 maximum amount per year and per account were also applicable for all American savers.

Then, on February 1, 2006, Mr. Ben Bernanke become the Chairman of the Federal Reserve and further tightened the screws on an already disappearing middle class, and pushed the majority of seniors into poverty.

From a young age, according to his biography, he was dreaming of becoming a millionaire. Once in the office, he immediately started catering to Wall Street, knowing very well that they would make him a millionaire, as they did his predecessor, Mr. Greenspan, who now has $10 million in personal wealth. Fascinated by Wall Street scams, Mr. Bernanke, when giving his lectures and speeches, started referring to Wall Street scams as "innovations."

To Mr. Bernanke, Wall Street scams that destroyed the American middle class and the USA economy became "innovations" (2 scams: "dot-com" and "subprime mortgages"). Immediately, using the power of his Chairmanship of the Federal Reserve, he started catering to Wall Street by outperforming his predecessor, Mr. Greenspan.

Mr. Bernanke made dramatic changes in I-bonds. He cut the maximum amount from $60,000 to $10,000, eliminated the fixed rate, and reduced the inflation rate to 1%.

For example, before, under Mr. Greenspan, $60,000 at 6%–8% interest in I-bonds was earning $3,600–$4,800 p.a. From now on, under Mr. Bernanke, $10,000 at 1% interest in I-bonds is earning only $100. That is why and how seniors, who live on fixed incomes, earning no interest from their savings, started living from their principals, soon exhausted it, and dropped into poverty.

Today, a record number of Americans are living in poverty or near the poverty line. The Bush administration added 10 million people to food stamps and the Obama administration added 20 million. Mr. Bernanke decimated the American middle class, pushed millions of seniors into poverty and did not save the USA economy.

The "0% interest rate" simply became Mr. Bernanke's scam fully designed to benefit banks and Wall Street. Many trillions of dollars that banks make from this "0% interest rate" scam simply are hoarded in bank coffers.

And why do bankers not invest these trillions of dollars back into the economy to create new jobs, products and services, as a "0% interest rate" was intended to do? Not a chance! Banks invested no money back into the economy. Why?

Very simple. Crooked bankers are very clever foxes; they need that money in bank coffers to pay themselves multimillion-dollar annual salaries and bonuses. If they put this money back into the economy, then where would they get trillions of dollars each year to pay themselves astronomical salaries?

To go back to the USA government, as they did in September of 2008, asking for another $700 billon bailout? Today, the USA government has no money, has $19 trillion in national debts, and is not going to bail them out again.

After Mr. Greenspan left the Federal Reserve, where his salary was $180,000 p.a., soon his fortune grew to a net of $10 million, a huge payback from Wall Street.

The same happened for Mr. Bernanke. Shortly, after he left his post, his boyhood dream to be a millionaire became a reality; in less than 1 year he had his first $2 million.

On October 9, 2013, a new Chairman of the Federal Reserve was appointed, Ms. Janet Yellen, a protégé of Mr. Bernanke. She not only continued Mr. Bernanke's "0% interest rate" scam, but made it even stiffer for the American savers.

She announced: "0 % interest rates will be here for a long time." It was music to the ears of the Wall Street crooks; excited, they went amok and drove the stock market up.

Scam #4.
The USA Government Doctrine "International Disorder"

The USA is today in peacetime—no more Cold War, the Iraq war is over, and the Afghanistan war is dwindling down. And the USA government started looking around the world to start another war. Why? So the joint venture between the USA government and their big donors—big companies, banks, and military industry—can keep going on and make their donors rich.

They found Ukraine. There on November 21, 2013, a peaceful demonstration started in the city plaza (the maidan in Ukrainian) against the government corruption. The USA interfered. They paid cash to thugs, fascists, and criminals; $1,000 per month in cash when an average salary in Ukraine is only $300.

Using drugs and drinking vodka, Nazi went on a rampage, became horrifying beasts and destroyed everything in their path. They burned government buildings and killed unarmed policemen and demonstrators. When demonstrators ran inside of buildings, Nazi threw Molotov cocktails inside and burned demonstrators alive. Those who tried to escape the inferno were finished outside with baseball bats by the raging beasts.

Just look at the news and see these raging Nazi in action. Everyone around them was terrified; that is why such a small violent minority overthrew the legitimate Ukrainian government. They were Nazi who went amok.

Scam #5.
Higher Education Scams

What was unthinkable not long ago, today has become a tragic reality. The American universities' presidents, and administrations all are involved in a scam— robbing their young students to pay themselves millions of dollars in annual salaries.

That is why today, student loans total over $1.1 trillion and the tragedy is, when they graduate, they have no jobs waiting for them.

It was not long ago when administration salaries in schools of higher education were small, $40,000–$60,000 and student tuitions even smaller. When I was in graduate school in the 1980s, tuitions were very small. I remember paying the tuitions with my credit card.

Scam #6.
Sports and Entertainment Industry Scams

Today professional athletes' salaries are in the many millions of dollars each. The irony is—they are paid such astronomical salaries for taking steroids to build their artificial muscles. Many also take recreational drugs that make them aggressive and violent on and off the fields.

In the 1970s, Muhammad Ali, the world heavyweight boxing champion, for the 1st time in the history of the sport received $1 million dollars for his fight with George Foreman in Congo, Kinshasa, on October 30, 1974.

The fight was a world event, the whole world was watching. And Ali paid 70% taxes on his $1 million, so he got actually less than $300,000. Ali never was on steroids or took any recreational drugs to make him strong and violent. Today, there is no one as legendary as Muhammad Ali was, but they all get paid hundreds of millions.

Before, tickets for all sports events were very cheap, with prices, often below $10. Currently, tickets can cost over $2,000 for popular games, without adding parking and concessions that also end up costing hundreds of dollars.

The same is true for the entertainment industry. Here, many movie stars and TV shows hosts who host the "trash shows," are drugs addicts, alcoholics, with a record of DUI, court appearances, fights, have bad behavior, and facing emotional problems. And for that they receive millions.

In 1963 there was a sensation Elizabeth Taylor, an international star, who received $1 million for her role in *Cleopatra, the Queen of Egypt.* She made history, as the 1st star who received $1 million for her role. Elizabeth did not want to play the role of Cleopatra, so when a Hollywood producer called her soliciting her to play the role, to get rid of him, as a joke, she commanded a $1 million salary. To her surprise, he agreed.

The point is, even such a glamorous, big star, as Elizabeth Taylor received a very small salary for her numerous roles. But today, there are no other stars like Ms. Taylor, but they still receive hundreds of millions for their diminutive roles.

Scam #7.
Private Prison Scams

Today, the American prison population is 2.2 million, or 25% of the entire world prison population. (The USA population is 316 million, or 4.5% of the world 7.2 billion population.) Private prisons are big business.

The USA government gave to private companies the responsibility to manage their prisons and is paying them an average $45,000–$50,000 per year to incarcerate an inmate in prison. The way to achieve the incentives of private companies, to get rich quick, is to have more prisoners. So they lobbied the USA policymakers to pass tougher laws for petty crimes committed by the average population.

Sometimes there are news stories about how private prison contractors were caught in scams where they paid judges and lawyers huge amounts of money to put more teenagers into jails for no crimes or petty crimes.

This occurred at the same time President Obama put not one Wall Street crook, banker, or private contractor into jail for their massive crimes of robbing trillions of dollars from the American population, for destroying the middle class, and for bringing the USA economy into a state of financial crisis. They are the big donors and hold every American politician squarely in their deep pockets. In short, it is more expensive to house an inmate than to give a child a decent education.

Scam #8.
Tax Scams

Tax rates keep dropping. In the 1950s–1960s the tax rates were 90%. Then, in the 1970s they dropped to 70%; then in the 1980s to 30%.

Today the top tax rate is 35%. The rich have no problem to avoid paying taxes, courtesy of numerous tax loopholes in the USA tax system; nor do they have difficulties to hide their money in many off-shores accounts and Swiss banks. As for American big corporations they pay little to no taxes.

Scam #9.
Miscellaneous Scams

The real estate scams involved selling old housing and condos that had no structural life left in them at inflated prices, for almost as much as the newly built homes. Car repair scams charged $120–180 per hour for labor, for doing a sub-standard job and installing used, not new, parts. Telephone and TV company scams, constantly increasing rates and cramming billings, and many more scams.

○ ○ ○

THE MORAL OF THE STORY

The USA economy is not recovering. Companies are announcing layoffs all the time, and their sales and profits are down. Why? Americans have no money to buy goods and services. Do not be indifferent.

Be enthusiastic about the life around you, participate in it, and try to change and improve things. You can change and improve the life around you, regardless of how small your contribution is. This is especially true today when everywhere you look, you see scams.

The Soviet Union disintegrated in 1991, changing the world into one single system—global capitalism.

And the race among 7.2 billon habitants started. Laws, regulations, dignity, and honor went out the window, only to be replaced by scams, schemes, lootings, and frauds.

Only one law exists—survival of the fittest, as in jungles. Everyone is running amok trying to "get rich quick from the thin air."

That is why new scams are popping up all the time. One of them, the biggest and the most damaging to the population, is the Federal Reserve scam of "0% interest rates." It is wiping out the backbone of this country—the middle class (the consumers). The middle class received no interest on their savings. Banks used middle class money for free and then lent back the money to the middle class at 4%–25% interest for mortgages, cars loans, private loans, student loans, and credit cards.

This "0% interest rate" scam also devastated seniors. With no earnings from interest accounts, seniors had to live on their principal monies, exhausted it, and now are living at or below the poverty line.

Who are the biggest beneficiaries of this "0% interest rate" scam? Banks are. From this scam, they made over $3 trillion that, according to the press, they are "hoarding and do not want to invest" in creating new jobs.

The reason bankers are hoarding this cash is to pay for their many million dollar salaries and bonuses. This time, they are afraid the USA government is not going to bail them out as it did in September 2008 to the tune of over $700 billion.

Another outrageous scam: low tax rates, tax loopholes, and tax avoidance by the rich and by large multi-national American corporations that explodes the nation's indebtedness which is now over $19 trillion.

All the while both political parties cannot agree on how to reduce and eliminate these monumental sovereign debts. Democrats want to raise taxes which are too low, especially on the rich. Republicans opposing raising taxes. instead, they want to cut spending. Meantime, tax receipts felling and the USA debts increasing.

Don't be apathetic regarding these scams. Instead, try to stop, change, and abolish scams that are robbing the population, the nation, eliminating the American middle class, and pushing millions into poverty.

President Bush added 10 million and President Obama added an additional 20 million Americans to the food stamps rolls. The American middle class disappeared. Today 1 in

2 Americans live in poverty or near the poverty line.

Prisons became private because it is more expensive to house an inmate than to give a child an education. The USA status changed— from a credit nation (before) to a debtor nation (today). Today the USA is the greatest debtor in the world, it has over $19 trillion ticking debts.

SHORT STORY

20

Why Couldn't the USA Recover from the Financial Crisis of September 2008? How Can the USA Recover from Today's Financial Crisis?

○　○　○

Why Couldn't the USA Recover from the Financial Crisis of September 2008?

This crisis of September 2008 was the 2nd worst economic crisis in American history. The 1st was the Great Depression of the 1930s. What triggered the Financial Crisis of 2008?

The 2 Wall Street scams—the "dot-com" and "subprime mortgages" that robbed the American middle class of all their life savings and pushed them into poverty.

The economy, having no more middle class consumers to spend money buying goods and services, stopped growing and crumbled. The USA government stepped in and bailed out Wall Street with $787 billion and put those unsustainable debts on the shoulders of already impoverished Americans.

There is high unemployment, foreclosures, skyrocketing cost of living, inflation, no security, 1.1 million are homeless, 2.2 million are in prison, growing population, millions of illegal immigrants competing for limited jobs, depletion of raw resources, an ecological holocaust, despair, and depression.

President Obama added 20 million Americans to food stamp list. Americans amassed $17 trillion in personal, mortgage, and credit card debt, and $1.1 trillion in student loans debts. Today, the USA national debt stands at $19 trillion, which is growing by $1.1 trillion per year. In just 5 years President Obama has added $9 trillion to the USA national debt.

The American middle class—the consumers—has disappeared. It has fallen onto the "have not" class, while at the same time 6.4 million new American millionaires and 400 new billionaires were created between 1995–2008 (whereas before 1995, it took 200 years to create 3.2 million millionaires in the USA).

Even more, the Soviet Union disintegrated and reshaped the world into one single system—the global capitalism, or the "get rich quick from thin air" mindset. It meant that the USA fearlessly is competing with 7.2 billion people for expensive oil, raw resources, and jobs.

American enterprises outsourced to poor foreign countries for cheaper labor. Hard industries that made things all but disappeared, with service industries that pay to the consumption of the goods once were made in the USA, but now made in China hiring workers at less pay. The population explosion put pressure on the earth, creating climate change with records of extreme weather, pollution, drought, flood, hot, cold, tornadoes, hurricanes, and forest fires. Billions of dollars are spent every year coping with extreme weather.

After the Financial Crisis of September 2008, the economy continued crumbling and the USA budget deficit has accelerated to $1.1 trillion annually. Why? Before 2008, Wall Street crooks invented 2 scams—the "dot.com" and "sub-prime mortgages"—scams to rob money from the USA population and the world.

The result was: the USA middle class lost all their pensions and IRAs and became poor. The foreign countries that bought Wall Street subprime mortgages (Iceland, Greece, Spain, Italy) are in dire economic straits, and 6.4 million Wall Street crooks became millionaires. The American population had no more money. So where do the Wall Street crooks get the money to continue "to get rich quick?" Answer is: from the USA government. It came to Wall Street's rescue with 2 government scams.

1st Scam

Federal Reserve "0% interest rate for savers." People put money into banks, and banks paid them 0% interest. Then the bank would loan back those peoples' money charging them 3%–25% interest rates.

Banks became rich from this scam and hoarded over $3 trillion dollars in their coffers to pay themselves billions in salaries and bonuses. Savers earned no interest on their money and seniors, who live on fixed incomes, fell into poverty.

2nd Scam

The World Peace Noble Laureate President Obama is drumming up military "World disorder." The Iraq war is over, the Afghanistan war is winding down, and President Obama is looking for another war to start. So, his big donors, military industry, banks, and big corporations continue making billions and trillions of dollars from the wars on other continents.

A recent example of this is the coup d'état in Ukraine, to create many more "war millionaires." Under President Obama, it is the first time in American history the USA annual budget deficit was over $1.1 trillion dollars.

Who is paying for this war? The USA Treasury. But the USA Treasury does not have money, the economy is in recession, and there is no more middle class or consumers to buy goods and services. No problem! The Federal Reserve is printing paper money to pay for war debts!

What Is the Solution?
What Is Needed for the USA Economy to Recover?

Solution #1

A noble USA President and selfless government are needed. A government which has some decency, dignity and honor, which will put their selfish personal enrichments below the USA economy, the nation, and the American people, and not bail out rich Wall Street capitalists at the expense of ordinary Americans.

History has witnessed that before; the USA had Noble Presidents such as Franklin D. Roosevelt and John F. Kennedy.

Solution #2

Eliminate the Wall Street casino, called "the stock market," and eliminate all lobbyists in Washington, D.C.

Solution #3

On top bracket raise income tax rate to 70%, as it was before. Today's income tax rates are extremely low. When for top bracket income tax in the 1960s were 90% and in the 1970s were 70%—the middle class was booming and blooming during those periods.

Raising taxes to 70% on top bracket is a good reason to resurrect the disappeared middle class, pay deficit, and boost the USA economy. Reform the whole tax system into a simple one, that does not have any loopholes and the propensity to cheat and avoid paying taxes.

Solution #4

The USA private health care must be transformed into the social health care, as it exists in all other countries in the world. So American physicians cannot became millionaires by performing not needed expensive tests, dangerous not needed operations, and prescribing dangerous drugs—all to became rich and millionaires.

Solution #5
Create and build national wealth that would create tens of millions of new jobs and boost the economy. Build new metropolitan cities, new transportation, many new superstructure to improve people quality of lives and cut down on environmental pollution.

Solution #6
Eliminate the influx of illegal immigrants by designing and implementing laws prohibiting businesses from hiring illegal immigrants. Impose high fees, penalties, and jail terms for breaking the law.

The USA is undergoing dramatic changes. It is no longer "a welcome nation of all immigrants." It is overpopulated, raw resources are exhausted, and unemployment is constant.

Solution #7
Cut population growth of 3.3 million per year through education and elimination of the tax discount for having many dependants.

Solution #8

Establish a government "think tank" of engineers to create innovations and find solutions on how to revitalize the USA economy. Engineers have creativity and skills to solve problems; they build national wealth and develop civilizations (not economists, not the Federal Reserve, and not financial consultants). What is engineering? Everything around us that is man-made and not created by nature—is engineering.

That is why in the former Soviet Union, all the Presidents and Politburo members were engineers. Even today in China (China is a capitalist country today), the President and his staff are all engineers; they know how to solve the country's problems, and how to create national wealth.

What Is a Noble President and a Noble Government?

The best example of a Noble President is Franklin D. Roosevelt, FDR, he was the only 4 term president.

He was an intellectual on the highest step of human development, "self-actualization." He served the nation and did not enrich himself and rich American capitalists. FDR declared during World War II: "There will be no war millionaires." He had dignity and honor, creativity on how to solve problems, he did not make Wall Street crooks his Secretaries of Treasury, and did not give the Federal Reserve free reign to run the economy and "find a solution" to the financial crisis.

FDR came from a rich family and was comfortable with what he had before becoming a President. During his Presidency, he did not add and was not expecting to add millions to his personal wealth after his presidency.

Not so with today's presidents. President Bill Clinton and Hillary Clinton have over $100 million fortune after Bill Clinton's presidency; Vice President Al Gore's fortune is at least $200 million after he left the office.

President Barack Obama is eager to join their club after his presidency ends. That is why he does everything Wall Street wants him to do for them. He even has Wall Street multimillionaires, as his Secretaries of Treasury. Analogy, as if to put 2 foxes to guard a chicken coop (the USA economy).

Obama let Wall Street run amok and let the Federal Reserve run a scam called "zero interest rates" that punished savers, impoverished the middle class, and pushed many seniors into poverty so big banks and big corporations could "get rich quick."

Today, banks from "zero interest rate" scams are sitting on trillions of dollars and hoarding it. The media was left wondering "Why don't banks invest this money into the economy to create jobs?" The answer is simple.

The reason bankers are sitting on trillions of dollars of cash is so they can pay themselves billions of dollars in salaries and bonuses every year. They know that they cannot ask the USA government for another bailout of $787 billion, as they did in September 2008. The USA government has no real money except printed money.

Why didn't President Obama put not one of the 6.4 million Wall Street crooks in jail for robbing over $5 trillion from the American middle class via the "dot-com" and "subprime-mortgages" scams?

The reason is that after his presidency, they are going to remunerate him with many of millions so he will join recent ex-Presidents and Vice Presidents in the multi-millionaire club.

Why hasn't the USA sunk yet from all these monumental problems and unsustainable debts?

Because it has 2 lifeboats: (1) The USA dollar is still a world currency, so other countries are still buying the USA's $19 trillion national debt; (2) The USA imports "brain drain" bright engineers and scientists from all over the world to create innovations and new technologies. What is going to happen when they leave the USA?

Soon the BRIC nations (Brazil, Russia, India, and China) are going to use their own currency to trade on the world market. Then, no one is going to buy USA dollars. What is going to happen to the USA and the $19 trillion national debt that is growing every day?

What is going to happen to the USA economy and to the well-being of the American people? A bankrupt USA will sink like the Titanic, and the American population will become impoverished.

o o o

THE MORAL OF THE STORY

Today the USA is in emergency survival mode. It cannot survive in this global capitalism system if it continues to be governed by the same type of presidents, policymakers, and government officials.

Today, to survive, the USA urgently needs a noble president and honest government officials who put the needs of the country above their selfish needs to become millionaires at the expense of the nation when holding positions in the USA government.

Today, as never before, the USA is facing many monumental problems from the outside world and from inside the country.

The outside world has changed dramatically— now all the world has only one single system—a global capitalist system to "get rich from thin air."

There are over 195 countries and 7.2 billion inhabitants in the world, among them is one country, the USA, with 316 million inhabitants competing for jobs and disappearing oil and raw resources. Everyone is in a hurry to have space get "rich quick."

A classic example is China: when China was a socialist country it lived below its means, did not trade on the world market, nor did it buy oil or raw resources on the world market, and it had few private cars and no millionaires.

Today, China is a global capitalist country. It has the fastest growing economy and today became the #1 economy in the world. It has 78 million cars and 2.4 million new millionaires.

The world has over 1 billion cars competing for oil and is steadily contributing to climate change and pollution.

To survive, the USA needs a noble President who knows how to solve national problems, is wise, has dignity and honor, and is not selfish and corrupt. A President who will put the country and the nation above his personal greed and enrichment. Who will stop rewarding his big donors: Wall Street, banks, big companies, and the military industry for his election and re-election with trillions of dollars from the USA Treasury at the expense of the American people.

Also, the USA needs a honest government to support and implement the President's policies.

Today the USA survival based on assumption that foreign countries are going to buy more and more of American debts every year. What is going to happen when they stop buying these debts? And there is no contingency plan for such catastrophe.

ACKNOWLEDGEMENTS

o o o

Many people directly or indirectly made many contributions to my books. But the biggest contributors, who made fundamental changes and altered the directions of my writing, were 2 men.

Dr. Samuel Oliner, who, after learning about my writing of 6 nonfiction books, encouraged me by all means to start with my short stories as the number 1 priority (not number 6, as I had planned before).

Harish Singhal who, after reading about my life, became buoyant and excited because my life has been a real thriller. He impel to write about it. Enthusiastically, he gave me confidence that my books would become successful.

ILLUSTRATION CREDITS

o o o

Front cover illustration: Light bulb illustration
    macrovector/ Dollar Photo Club
Copyright page, back cover and spine: Sun symbol
    SCA-Graphics/Dollar Photo Club
Short Story #1
    Scott Maxwell/ Shutterstock
Short Story #2
    Aliasching/Dollar Photo Club
Short Story #3
    Kheng Guan Toh/Dollar Photo Club
Short Story #4
    Sam72/Shutterstock
Short Story #5
    SkyLine/Dollar Photo Club
Short Story #6
    Concept w/Shutterstock
Short Story #7
    Evgeny Skidanov/Dollar Photo Club
Short Story #8
    Kurhan/Dollar Photo Club
Short Story #9
    Volkankutlubay/Dollar Photo Club
Short Story #10
    Andrey Burmakin/Dollar Photo Club

Short Story #11

Everett Historical/Shutterstock

Short Story #12

a) Mega Pixal/Shutterstock

b) Dirk Ercken/Shutterstock

Short Story #13

a) Iculig/Dollar Photo Club

b) Michele Paccione/Shutterstock

Short Story #14

a) Krasimira Nevenova/Dollar Photo Club

b) Manczurov/Shutterstock

Short Story #15

a) rSnapshotPhoto/Shutterstock

b) Alienforce/Dollar Photo Club

Short Story #16

a) Lynea/Shutterstock

b) Jason and Bonnie Grower/Shutter Stock

Short Story #17

Everett Collection/Shutterstock

Short Story #18

Ax photobox//Dollar Photo Club

Short Story #19

Nickylarson74/Dollar Photo Club

Short Story #20

Razihusin/Shutterstock

Short Stories #1–20 Owl at a book pile

Olandsfokus/Dollar Photo Club

"The Forces of Innovations...Conflict?,"
an article by Carissa Giblin, *The Florida
Engineering Journal*

THE AUTHOR'S, ALLA P. GAKUBA, BSCE, MAS, PhD, CONTRIBUTIONS TO ENGINEERING, TO NATIONAL WEALTH, AND TO WOMEN:

The Forces of Innovation...Conflict?

BY CARISSA GIBLIN, ARTICLE PROVIDED BY THE SOCIETY OF WOMEN ENGINEERS.

FLORIDA ENGINEERING JOURNAL, JANUARY 2004.

Many people ask Alla Gakuba how she innovates. She responds that she does not remember inventing something under normal circumstances; that is, without huge external and internal pressures. And it seems to be true. She came across a study while writing her dissertation for her PhD at George Washington University. The study surveyed thousands. of inventors asking them what factors were responsible for their innovations. The conclusion was great stress and pressure.

When Alla came to Baltimore, Maryland, in the beginning of the 1970s from the then USSR, she faced several environmental factors that created this pressure. There were few women engineers at the time. English was a new language to her. She knew only the metric system. Her husband was a physician working long hours, and they had two small children. It was the peak of the Cold War, and American engineers were paying close attention to Russian science and technology.

To her surprise, she was soon hired as a structural engineer. Never mind that Alla was not yet an engineer and that her English was only 4 months old. She had familiarized herself with the state building codes for a few days when the Chief Engineer told her her first project would be designing a three span bridge over a ramp—completely on her own.

He handed her a field drawing depicting the location of the ramp. As she took the drawing, dizziness overwhelmed her. "How in the world am I going to design it?" ran through her head. In her memory she went back to engineering school in expectation to retrieve some information about the design. She could recall none. In school she took math, physics, chemistry, static, kinematics, dynamics, strength of material, and reinforced concrete and steel. There was no trace of bridge design. She walked back to her office in despair.

On her way home that evening she stopped at the bridge site and examined the parapets, decks, piers, columns, and footings of the nearby ramps. The next day she had a lot of ideas on how to design the bridge. Looking at the field drawing of the ramp, she recognized that she needed to know the soil pressure under the bridge. Randomly, she sketched a dozen of soil borings.

When she gave her sketch to the soil department and asked for pressure measurements, they took her seriously and asked when she needed the information. She realized then she was on the right track. She started focusing on the bridge design. Alla decided to stay, and the pressure was on.

Alla was able to draw upon her engineering problem-solving skills and determination to succeed. She divided the bridge into separate structures. Using common sense and applying math, physics, and strength of materials, she designed each component one by one. All the pieces fit together as a puzzle, and it became the bridge. The company assembled a team of engineers to check her design and they were astounded at the calculations she used. She told them that no one gave her guidance so she invented each of the calculations.

Her design was accepted 100%. As they learned how simple it was, her calculation methods became standard in the company. Alla had created her own way of designing instead of copying the standard processes. Some time later, Alla learned bridge design traditionally involved a team of engineers each specializing in a particular structure. The company had given her the whole bridge to design to gain insight on Russian engineering and also to limit her success as the only female engineer in the company. In the end the company was so impressed, they started searching for another woman engineer.

Alla's next contribution involved an I-95, ten span bridge with four ramps over the Patapsco River in downtown Baltimore. She was given an opportunity to design this bridge alone. This time, the company trusted and believed in her; otherwise they would not have put all their eggs into one basket. And she lived up to their expectations. Not only did she design the bridge and ramps, but she also introduced a new foundation design. It required 30% less construction materials than standard foundations. The revolutionary aspect was that Alla's foundation designs took just one page of calculations for each pier.

Usually the design of foundation for each pier required computer programs followed by 70–80 pages of hand calculations. Her calculations and drawings were wrapped up and sent to an outside consulting company to check if they were correct.

Several months later, the consultants' hundreds of pages of computer printouts and calculations produced the same result as the innovations that Alla had calculated on one page.

Later, Alla was given a challenge to find a solution to a spiral design for 5.5 miles of aerial structure for the Baltimore Subway.

Only later did she learn that before approaching her, the company advertised in professional magazines across the country for engineers who could design a spiral for the subway. The company received no response. This was because no one had designed this before and no one wanted to risk their career.

So, Alla took on the project. She started with a blank piece of paper. The chief engineer told her about two French books about the new Paris subway sections housed in the Library of Congress in Washington, DC. She retrieved the books along with a French-English Civil Engineering dictionary. (She knew some French, but not civil engineering French.) The information only reinforced that what is applicable in Paris was not applicable in Baltimore. Also, the books were not about calculations and design of a spiral. Instead, they were about the philosophy, problems, and approach to design.

In the end, she made her own invention and found the solution for a spiral design. She calculated one span by long hand. Then, it was very simple to mirror her calculations and run the remaining 550 or so spans through the computer. The company wrote that Alla found the solution for spiral design of the aerial structure and that they considered it to be the most difficult engineering design. As for Alla, the spiral design was a nightmare that she cannot forget easily.

Alla cannot attribute the above contributions to herself only. She was a product of time, place, and circumstances. The time was the 1970s, which were the best technological years in her generation. The place was the US where equal employment opportunity laws were taking shape. She was a Russian in the US during the Cold War, where the great technological and political competitions for the dominance of the world were taking place between the two countries. She was given opportunity and responsibility and she lived up to their expectations. If Alla had stayed in the USSR, she doubts that she would have produced such contributions. In her opinion, there is no incentive to innovate in a familiar supportive environment. There must be a pressure.

Next, Alla managed the construction of the Baltimore Subway.

Her next objective was to enlarge her knowledge and became a better person. She received her Master's Degree from John Hopkins University where professors and students encouraged her to earn a PhD so she could become a role model for other women. She did. She received her Doctoral degree from George Washington University with a major in Management of Science, Technology, and Innovations. She was the first woman to graduate in this field. Her dissertation was ranked among the top 5% of the 250–300 dissertations which have been written in the last 15 years.

Alla Gakuba, PhD is a business analyst and consultant in Tampa, Florida. She earned her Bachelor of Science in Civil Engineering from Odessa Civil Engineering University in the former Soviet Union.

(Reprint of this article was granted by *The Florida Engineering Journal* on January 19, 2015.)

HAVE YOU READ? BOOKS BY
ALLA P. GAKUBA, BSCE, MAS, PhD

ALLA P. GAKUBA, BSCE, MAS, PhD

WHAT IS LIFE? WHAT IS HAPPINESS?

Book 1 in the trilogy: motivational nonfiction short stories to teach logic, creativity, new skills, and self-esteem that would change readers lives

A PERSON IS A PRODUCT OF TIME, PLACE, AND CIRCUMSTANCES

Book 2 in the trilogy: motivational nonfiction short stories to teach logic, creativity, new skills, and self-esteem that would change readers lives

ALLA P. GAKUBA, BSCE, MAS, PhD

ALLA P. GAKUBA, BSCE, MAS, PhD

How to Design Innovations and Solve Business and Personal Problems

Book 3 in the trilogy: motivational nonfiction short stories to teach logic, creativity, new skills, and self-esteem that would change readers lives

Available wherever books sold

www.ingramcontent.com/pod-product-compliance
Lightning Source LLC
Chambersburg PA
CBHW031118020426
42333CB00012B/136